The Political Rise of Donald J. Trump

The Political Rise of Donald J. Trump

HOW THE NEWS MEDIA & POLITICAL CLASS TRIED TO STOP IT & WHY THEY FAILED

• • •

Nicholas Kadar

ISBN: 1537049054
ISBN 13: 9781537049052

For Nicola

If—

• • •

If you can keep your head when all about you
    Are losing theirs and blaming it on you,
If you can trust yourself when all men doubt you,
    But make allowance for their doubting too;
If you can wait and not be tired by waiting,
    Or being lied about, don't deal in lies,
Or being hated, don't give way to hating,
    And yet don't look too good, nor talk too wise:

If you can dream—and not make dreams your master;
    If you can think—and not make thoughts your aim;
If you can meet with Triumph and Disaster
    And treat those two impostors just the same;
If you can bear to hear the truth you've spoken
    Twisted by knaves to make a trap for fools,
Or watch the things you gave your life to, broken,
    And stoop and build 'em up with worn-out tools:

If you can make one heap of all your winnings
    And risk it on one turn of pitch-and-toss,
And lose, and start again at your beginnings

And never breathe a word about your loss;
If you can force your heart and nerve and sinew
    To serve your turn long after they are gone,
And so hold on when there is nothing in you
    Except the Will which says to them: 'Hold on!'

If you can talk with crowds and keep your virtue,
    Or walk with Kings—nor lose the common touch,
If neither foes nor loving friends can hurt you,
    If all men count with you, but none too much;
If you can fill the unforgiving minute
    With sixty seconds' worth of distance run,
Yours is the Earth and everything that's in it,
    And—which is more—you'll be a Man, my son!

Rudyard Kipling

Contents

If— · vii

Part I   How the News Media Creates
               False Social Narratives · · · · · · · · · · · · · · · · · 1
Introduction What couldn't.....happened · · · · · · · · · · · · · · · · 3
Chapter 1   Media Bias & Democracy · · · · · · · · · · · · · · · 13
Chapter 2   Truth Rarely Catches Up With the Lie · · · · · · · · 21
Chapter 3   How the News Media Biases News · · · · · · · · · · · 29
Chapter 4   Creating Falsehoods by Checking Facts · · · · · · · · 49

Part II   Into The Meat Grinder · · · · · · · · · · · · · · · · · 63
Chapter 5   Trump Announces his Candidacy · · · · · · · · · · · · 65
Chapter 6   Trump versus a War Hero · · · · · · · · · · · · · · · 73
Chapter 7   Trump versus a Female Reporter · · · · · · · · · · · · 77
Chapter 8   Candidates Exit the Race · · · · · · · · · · · · · · · · 82
Chapter 9   Muslims Celebrating 9/11 in New Jersey · · · · · · · 87
Chapter 10   San Bernardino and the Muslim Ban · · · · · · · · · · 93
Chapter 11   Final Salvos Fizzle · 98
Chapter 12   With Egg on their Faces · · · · · · · · · · · · · · · · · 101

Part III   The Race Begins
              A: February Winnows The Field · · · · · · · · · · · · 105
Chapter 13   Anything you can do Trump can do better · · · · · 107
Chapter 14   The Iowa Caucuses: February 1, 2016 · · · · · · · · · · · 113
Chapter 15   The New Hampshire Primary: February 9, 2016 · · · 117
Chapter 16   The South Carolina Primary: February 20, 2016 · · 122
Chapter 17   Blitzkrieg · 133
Chapter 18   The News Media's *Faux* Racist · · · · · · · · · · · · · 141

Part III   B: March Madness · 145
Chapter 19   The 'Stop-Trump' Movement · · · · · · · · · · · · · · 147
Chapter 20   Inciting Violence: the New anti-Trump Narrative · ·156
Chapter 21   Ides of March · 164
Chapter 22   More Violence · 169
Chapter 23   From Violence to the Gutter · · · · · · · · · · · · · · · 174
Chapter 24   Work It Baby · 177

Part III   C: April Fool · 183
Chapter 25   Then It Got Worse · 185
Chapter 26   Home Sweet Home · 193
Chapter 27   The Northeast Primaries · · · · · · · · · · · · · · · · ·200
Chapter 28   Indiana: Cruz's Last Stand · · · · · · · · · · · · · · · 205
Chapter 29   The Last Hurrah · 213
Chapter 30   It's All Over Now, Baby Blue · · · · · · · · · · · · · · · 220

Part IV   The Denouement · 223
Chapter 31   The Aftermath · 225
Chapter 32   Events, Dear Boy · 233
Chapter 33   Trump Triumphant: the Republican National
              Convention · 242

Part V   *Why the News Media & Political Class*
              Failed to Stop Trump · 259
Chapter 34   Why the News Media Failed: Questions of Fact · · 261
Chapter 35   Why the Political Class Failed: A Question of
              Leadership · 283
Chapter 36   Trump's Appeal: A Question of Identity · · · · · · · 301
Conclusion   Trump v. Status Quo · 305

PART I

How the News Media Creates
False Social Narratives

• • •

What couldn't…..happened

• • •

There's no use trying.
One can't believe impossible things.

ON MAY 3, 2016 DONALD J. Trump won the Indiana Republican primary, and became the Republican Party's presumptive nominee for President of the United States. It was one of the most extraordinary political event in American history.

No one believed Trump would even run for President much less that he could win the Republican Party's nomination. So when Trump did announce his candidacy on June 16, 2015 no one took him seriously. Jeb Bush, the prohibitive favorite to win the nomination, repeatedly told reporters, *"Donald Trump is not a serious candidate"*.

Known as The Donald, Trump was a larger-than-life, thrice-married, flamboyant billionaire who had made his fortune in the New York real estate market, and owned or had owned several of the city's iconic landmarks, which had the name TRUMP emblazoned on them in red or Gold. He had a reputation for being a winner, for completing projects ahead of schedule and under budget. He was the author of the best-selling book, *The Art of the Deal*, but best known today as the star of NBC's reality show, *The Apprentice*, that still enjoyed high ratings after fourteen seasons. The show was indelibly associated in the public's mind with Trump saying to one of the contestants at the end of each episode, *"You're fired"*.

Everyone treated Trump's candidacy as a joke—a clever gimmick to boost the Trump brand. The *Huffington Post* told readers it would treat Trump's campaign as entertainment:

> *"After watching and listening to Donald Trump since he announced his candidacy for president, we have decided we won't report on Trump's campaign as part of the Huffington Post's political coverage. Instead, we will cover his campaign as part of our Entertainment section."*[1]

A poll taken shortly after Trump announced his candidacy had Trump last with 1% of the vote: Jeb Bush was leading with 22%. Two-thirds of the people polled said they would never vote for Trump, and when asked if he would vote for Trump if Trump won the nomination, Jeb Bush confidently predicted, *"Donald will not be the nominee of the Republican Party"*.

Even three months after Trump announced his candidacy, when he was leading in every poll, the first question *New York Times* contributor John Harwood asked Trump at the Third Republican Debate in Boulder, Colorado hosted by CNBC was:

---

1 http://www.huffingtonpost.com/entry/a-note-about-our-coverage-of-donald-trumps-campaign_us_55a8fc9ce4b0896514d0fd66

"Let's be honest, is this the comic book version of a presidential campaign?"

Harwood made a fool of himself with that question because it advertised to the world that he didn't have a clue about what was going on. What was unfolding before his eyes was simply too far outside his experience, and Harwood couldn't make sense of it. No one could.

Trump had never held or even run for elected office before. He was one of seventeen candidates, and running against the best and most experienced candidates the Republicans had fielded in years. Nine were sitting or former governors;[2] five were sitting or former U.S. Senators.[3] Carly Fiorina, the former CEO of Hewlett Packard, had run for the U.S. Senate from California, and was an experienced campaigner. Ben Carson, a retired neurosurgeon, was the only other candidate besides Trump who had never run for elected office before.

Trump was funding his own campaign. He had a threadbare organization, no campaign infrastructure, and spent little on advertising. He had no pollsters, no handlers, no speech writers, no advisors. He was not an accomplished public speaker. He spoke off the cuff at rallies without a teleprompter, often in incomplete sentences. What he said regularly created an outcry from his opponents, the political establishment, and the news media. Yet people turned up in their tens of thousands at his rallies. Many drove long distances and waited for up to eight hours in sweltering heat and then in the rain or freezing cold temperatures to hear him speak. What was going on?

---

2 Chris Christie (NJ); Bobby Jindal (LA); John Kasich (OH); Scott Walker (WI); and former governors Jeb Bush (FL); Jim Gilmore (VA); Mike Huckabee (AR); Rick Perry (TX); George Pataki (NY).
3 Ted Cruz (TX); Lindsay Graham (SC); Rand Paul (KY); Marco Rubio (FL); and former Senator Rick Santorum (PA).

Jeb Bush, a popular former governor of Florida, and younger brother of President George W. Bush, was the prohibitive favorite from the start. His campaign posters had the slogan JEB! without his last name: it was, to emphasize that he was his own man, with his own ideas, and wasn't asking people to vote for him based on his last name.

Bush had amassed a war chest of $140 million from donors before he entered the race—the day before Trump. In just a month, Trump had overtaken Bush in a national poll, and for the first time narrowly led Bush by 17% to 14%. It was a lead Trump would never relinquish except for two weeks in the beginning of November, when some polls had Ben Carson in a statistical tie with Trump. But Trump catapulted back into the lead again after the terrorist attack on Paris on November 13, 2015, and led the race in every poll thereafter.

What made the Trump phenomenon so extraordinary was not the improbability of an outsider, who had never held or even run for office, beating such a large and talented field of experienced politicians. It was the fierceness and breadth of the opposition against which Trump won front-runner status, held on to his lead to the end, and eventually won the Republican Party's nomination for President. He towered over all opposition by the sheer force of his personality that the comedian Dennis Miller described as a 'force of nature'.

Trump was opposed by the news media, and the cable news networks ran negative stories denouncing Trump every hour, every weekday throughout the primary campaign—not just CNN and MSNBC, the liberal networks, but also Fox News, the bastion of conservatism in cable news from which most Republicans get their political news. Fox news was promoting Marco Rubio, a young, attractive, first-term Senator from the key battleground state of Florida. It interviewed Rubio regularly to give him maximum exposure to its large Republican audience, and denounced Trump no less stridently than CNN and MSNBC.

But Trump's fiercest critics were the Conservatives in his own party: their opposition to Trump was unrestrained and unrelenting. They predicted that if Trump was nominated, Republicans would lose many House and Senate races, lose their majority in the Senate and maybe even the House, and hand a landslide victory to Hillary Clinton, who would appoint liberal justices to the Supreme Court. It would mean the end of the Republican Party, and the American way of life as we know it.

The Conservative's opposition to Trump is difficult to overstate. Conservatives stated publicly that they would leave the Republican Party if Trump was nominated, and after the voting began a plethora of anti-Trump movements organized SuperPacs to try to stop Trump.

Trump was denounced as a racist, bigot, xenophobe, sexist, and misogynist; he was accused of inciting violence at his rallies, of being anti-immigrant, of mocking a disabled reporter and using vulgar, obscene language in public. He was called a fraud and a cancer on conservatism; the suitability of his temperament and character were called into question. Elected Republicans stated in public that they could never vote for him. Party officials met formally to discuss how Trump could be stopped; Republican donors funded SuperPacs to oppose him, and spent $75 million airing 64,000 negative advertisements against Trump. The conservative radio talk show host Rush Limbaugh summed it all up:

"Now folks, the conventional wisdom is that Trump is scum, that Trump is a reprobate, that Trump is dangerous, that Trump is obscene, Trump's insane, Trump's a lunatic, Trump's dangerous, Trump's got to go."[4]

None of it worked. Five of Trump's opponents dropped out of the race before the first vote was ever cast at the Iowa caucuses on February 1, 2016.[5] Three more dropped out after the Iowa caucuses,[6] and three more a week later, after the New Hampshire primary.[7] Bush dropped out after the South Carolina primary on February 20, 2016, and Marco Rubio after he lost the Florida primary by double digits on March 15, 2016.

Cruz and Kasich stayed in the race, even after they had no chance of winning the nomination outright. They were urged to stay in, and continued to be funded for the express purpose of stopping Trump from getting the 1237 delegates needed to win the nomination on the first ballot. The plan was to contest the nomination at the Republican Convention in Cleveland, and for Cruz or Kasich or some outsider to win the nomination on the second, third or even the fourth ballot as Abraham Lincoln had done in 1860.

Neither the Media nor the political establishment gave up easily. Each networks' 'numbers men' told the public how many delegates Trump was likely get in the remaining primaries, and consistently concluded that—even on the most optimistic assumptions about the

---

4 http://www.rushlimbaugh.com/daily/2015/12/08/how_donald_trump_plays_the_media

5 Rick Perry (Sept. 11, 2015), Scott Walker (Sept. 21, 2015), Bobby Jindal (Nov. 17, 2015), Lindsay Graham (Dec. 21, 2015), and George Pataki (Dec. 29, 2015).

6 Mike Huckabee (Feb. 1, 2016), Rick Santorum (Feb. 1, 2016), Rand Paul (Feb 3, 2016).

7 Chris Christie (Feb. 10, 2016), Carly Fiorina (Feb. 10, 2016), and Jim Gilmore (Feb 12, 2016).

outcome of the remaining primaries—Trump was highly unlikely to get the 1237 delegates he needed to win outright.

"*Possible? Yes, but very unlikely*," CNN's John King told his audience almost every day.

Then it abruptly ended on May 3, 2016, the day of the Indiana Primary. That was Cruz's firewall—his last chance to stop Trump. Cruz's campaign, and anti-Trump SuperPacs spent $5.3 million on negative advertising against Trump in the state. Cruz gave it his all, but Trump won Indiana by 17%, and got over 50% of the vote. Cruz dropped out of the race that night, and after he did, Reince Priebus, the RNC chairman, immediately declared Trump the presumptive nominee of the Republican Party. It took everyone by surprise. Kasich canceled a scheduled event in Washington, and dropped out of the race the following day.

But the Media didn't let up on its attacks, and tried to minimize the significance of his victory. Trump may have won the nomination but couldn't win a general election became the narrative. A general election is very different from the primaries: to win the general election Trump would have to unite the Republican Party, and he had alienated too many people to do that. The rhetoric continued, but everyone knew it was all over. All that remained were the formalities: the voting in the eight remaining primaries, and the nomination at the Republican Convention in Cleveland on July 18, 2016.

What happened? How did Trump win Republican Party's nomination and win it by more votes that any candidate in the history of the Republican Party—by more votes than Eisenhower, Nixon, and even Ronald Reagan? Why did all the screaming of Conservatives like Ben Ferguson, Erik Erickson, and Mark Levin, and the rationalizations of Karl Rove, Bill Kristol, David Brooks, and other political 'consultants' and 'strategists' and 'analysts' have so little effect? Why did the Stop-Trump, Never-Trump, Anyone-but-Trump, and every other anti-Trump movement fizzle out? How could the news media and entire American political class have got it so wrong and have had so little effect on the Trump candidacy?

As he so often does, Rush Limbaugh best summed up the situation in his own inimitable way:

> *"Despite it all they can't take him out. They can't humiliate him. They can't embarrass him. They can't diminish his support. They're powerless, and this has them in a panic. The media that can make-or-break anybody cannot touch Trump, and every time they try, all they do is make him bigger. They can't explain this. They are frustrated to no end, and so are both political parties who rely on the media to be the great equalizer in all of this."*[8]

It was obvious that no one in the Media had figured out what about Trump and his message caused people to flock to his rallies, feel empowered, and resist the efforts of so many groups in the country to demonize Trump, tarnish his message, and kill his candidacy. Was Trump simply offering better policy choices for the electorate than his competitors or was there something more transformational about his message that challenged the accepted paradigm of our age—globalism and multiculturalism—and that restored a national imaginary, a self-image Americans were yearning to regain?

---

8 Rush Limbaugh, supra note 4 (page 11).

This book makes the case that Trump won the nomination because time and time again events proved that he was none of things he was portrayed by the media to be, nor exploiting the anger of an electorate disillusioned with Washington. Rather, Trump was a transformational leader who was espousing quintessentially American values, and empowering people by making them feel part of something bigger than themselves and their own self-interests.

This book is also a story about the news media's role in all this. It makes the case that the news media failed to kill Trump's candidacy because it overreached: how it portrayed Trump and what it said about world events during the primaries were simply not true; and the gist of what Trump was saying *was* true, even if what he said was terminologically inexact or incorrect or contained some factual inaccuracies. But above all, the news media couldn't take Trump down because, despite all his negatives in polling data, Trump was espousing quintessentially American values that resonated with many Americans.

The news media's attempt to kill the Trump candidacy raises additional questions, serious and fundamental, about the news media and our democracy. Is the media providing us with independent, trustworthy information or delivering self-interested propaganda to affirm the views of its audience, and creating a social reality it would like to be true?[9] Are the media's self-appointed fact-checkers, who presume to tell the public what is 'true' and not true, checking the news evenhandedly? Are they actually checking the accuracy of what news items mean or quibbling over definitions and statistics to sway public opinion to their points of view?

---

9 See generally, Bill Kovach & Tom Rosenstiel, The Elements of Journalism, Three Rivers Press, N.Y. 2014.

These are important questions to ask for a country that presumes to lead the free world at a time of widespread institutional instability and personal insecurity throughout the world. The answers to them are intertwined, as can be gleaned from the reasons given by the noted British historian, Paul Johnson, for endorsing Trump, and for calling political correctness *"one of the most dangerous intellectual afflictions ever to attack mankind"*.

Among the many books Johnson has written is an engaging, almost loving history of America and its people, which may explain why he views the Trump candidacy as *"just what America needs"*:

"Nowhere has PC [political correctness] *been more triumphant than in the U.S.,"* Johnson wrote. *"This is remarkable, because America has traditionally been the home of vigorous, outspoken, raw and raucous speech. From the early 17th century… America has been a land of unrestricted comment on anything–until recently. Now the U.S. has been inundated with PC inquisitors, and PC poison is spreading worldwide in the Anglo zone.*

For these reasons it's good news that Donald Trump is doing so well in the American political primaries. He is vulgar, abusive, nasty, rude, boorish and outrageous. He is also saying what he thinks and, more important, teaching Americans how to think for themselves again."[10]

Whether the reader agrees with Johnson or the answers this book offers, the questions about leadership and the news media raised by Trump's nomination urgently need to be addressed and widely discussed in this country.

---

10 http://www.forbes.com/sites/currentevents/2016/03/23/when-excess-is-a-virtue/#77bbb83b34b5

CHAPTER 1

Media Bias & Democracy

• • •

"Whenever the people are well-informed, they can
be trusted with their own government…"

THOMAS JEFFERSON

FOR A DEMOCRACY TO SURVIVE there has to be a free and independent press—independent, that is, of what it covers. Independence doesn't mean neutrality: we want journalists to have opinions about what they cover; we want to hear their ideas, as ideas drive progress and change. But the press can only be wedded to a cause, an issue, a policy, a principle, an idea, not a person, a party or a faction: and it must be wedded to it for valid, transparent and articulable reasons, and cannot be dishonest about where its sympathies lie.[11]

The news media's coverage of Donald Trump's primary campaign was so blatantly biased as to border on farce. In June, 2016, the Media Research Center reported that the network evening newscasts devoted four times more airtime to controversies involving Donald

---

11 Kovach & Rosenstiel, supra note 9 at 150-168 (page 13)

Trump than Hillary Clinton.[12] On August 3, 2016, following the Republican and Democrat National Conventions, the Center's director, Rich Noyes, reported that CNN's morning program *New Day* gave 200 times the coverage to Trump controversies than to the $400 million cash delivered to Iran in an unmarked cargo plane on the day four American hostage were released, creating the impression that a ransom had been paid.[13]

A parent who had lost a child to terrorism spoke at each party's National Convention. Khizr Khan, a Muslim immigrant from Pakistan whose son was a U.S. soldier and killed in Afghanistan by a suicide bomber, denounced Trump at the Democrat Convention, and his denunciation aired repeatedly by the news media for days. Patricia Smith, whose son was killed in the terrorist attack on the U.S. consulate in Benghazi denounced Hillary Clinton at the Republican Convention, and the press denounced her for doing it. The Media Research Center reported that the three big networks, ABC, CBS and NBC devoted 50 times more coverage to Khizr Khan than Patricia Smith notwithstanding that Trump had nothing to do with the death of Khan's son, who was killed in 2001, whereas Clinton was directly implicated in Smith's son's death.

There is, of course, nothing wrong with the news media criticizing a political candidate: we want 'opinion journalism'. But there is a difference between opinion journalism and partisan propaganda; [14] between expressing an opinion and asserting it as a fact; between arguing from facts to conclusions, and reaching conclusions by distorting or making up facts or leaving them out. Opinion journalism

---

12 http://newsbusters.org/blogs/nb/rich-noyes/2016/06/20/tv-news-feasts-trump-controversies-while-ignoring-hillarys-scandals

13 http://www.mrc.org/

14 Kovach & Rosenstiel, supra note 9 at 146 (page 13).

does not select, censor, misrepresent or distort facts, take them out of context, or invent facts to give events a desired meaning and create false social realities.

Authentic opinion journalists, unlike propagandists, are willing to look at things from multiple points of view; to recognize that there are often several valid interpretations of events. They avoid oversimplifications, false equivalences, and distortions caused by 'balancing' points of views when there may be more than two sides to a story, or giving every point of view equal weight.[15]

Opinion journalists divulge all the evidence, and explain why a preferred interpretation of events is the best one. They engage their opponents' strongest arguments, not their weakest.[16] Opinion journalists seek to persuade, not to manipulate. They try to make sense of the news, and don't pretend to be reporting it.[17] Good opinion journalism is incompatible with 'political correctness'.

But before the press can make sense of the news, it has to report it, and report it in a way that provides people with the information they need to govern themselves. That means giving them accurate, reliable, and complete accounts of events in the world, and that in turn means the news media has to get its facts straight, verify them, and put them into proper context. Without that, the news media cannot fulfill its most important job, which is to provide the public with the information it needs to detect lies, because without such information there can be no liberty for any community.[18] These are

---

15 Id. at 155-57

16 Id. at 143

17 Id. at 140-43

18 Id.

not easy tasks at the best of times, and now is not the best of times for the news media.

Reporting the news has been described as a 'reality-making activity' and not merely a 'reality-describing' task.[19] News is narrative: the meaning conveyed by a news story goes beyond the facts reported, and depends on how the story is told. Reporters, like everyone else, are biased by their experiences, culture and political ideologies, and can never be completely objective about what they report. Therefore, their methods have to be objective, rigorous, and transparent.[20] They must strip from their accounts of the news rumor, innuendo, and 'spin', and correct and update any information they present.[21] How many reporters today do that?

The news media today provides the public neither unfiltered news, nor good opinion journalism, because it has become politically partisan and ideologically polarized, and is also driven by ratings. Their reports are selective; they cater to a targeted audience, and interpret the news to reinforce their audience's preconceptions. They make political operatives part of the team that reports the news. They define problems in terms of conflicts, drama and personalities, present policy options in terms of just a few options, and falsely balance claims as if they were equally validity.[22] They slant what they report; they raise selective questions about it; they select sources that express their own point of view, but represent them as objective.

---

19 Marilyn Lester, Generating Newsworthiness: The Interpretive Construction of Public Events. Am. Soc. Rev. 1980;45: 984-94
20 Kovach & Rosenstiel, supra note 9 at 97-129 (page 13).
21 Id. at 58
22 Id. at 109

The news media makes two decisions that necessarily intervene between what happens in the world and what is reported and discussed as news: [23]

1. A decision about what is news;
2. A decision about how to present it.

The news media does not make these decisions in order to advance democracy: they make them in a calculated way for economic reasons,[24] and to advance the political preferences and agendas of their organizations and the audiences to which they cater.[25] For example, the Pew Research Center's Project for Excellence in Journalism reported that in 2007

> *"MSNBC made the key decision to reprogram itself as a liberal counterweight to the Fox News Channel's conservative nighttime line up* [and became]*by far the most opinionated of the three networks, with nearly 90% of its primetime coverage coming in the form of opinion or commentary"*.[26]

Biased reporting of news, like political correctness, insidiously manipulates public opinion by controlling the information the public receives and the viewpoints to which it is exposed. It undermines trust in government and public officials, and diminishes social capital because to control the information people get, or how they get

---

23 Marilyn Lester, supra note 19.

24 See e.g. Robert W. McChesney & Victor Packard (eds): Will the last reporter please turn out the lights: the collapse of journalism and what can be done about it. The New Press, 2011.

25 Kovach & Rosenstiel, supra note 9 at 61-68 (page 13)

26 http://www.stateofthemedia.org/2013/special-reports-landing-page/the-changing-tv-news-landscape

it, is largely to control what they think and believe, what ideas they have, and what opinion they hold—and that is why the first thing to-talitarian governments do on coming to power is to seize control of the news media. That is also why Paul Johnson was not exaggerating when he said that political correctness was *"one of the most dangerous intellectual afflictions ever to attack mankind"*[27]—because it causes self-censorship and stifles frees speech.

The reporting of political news today is biased because it is driven by the agenda of a partisan news media, and is influenced by which political party happens to be in power. The news media is no longer content to endorse or criticize political candidates and public policies: the American news media provides the public disproportionate accounts of events and slants the news to impugn candidates they don't like and to promote policies they favor. That is why, for example, the *New York Times*, which supports and promotes President Obama's policies, referred to the atroc-ity that killed over 80 innocent bystanders in Nice, France as a *"Truck Attack in Nice"*, and not a terrorist attack[28]—to be consistent with the vocabulary the Obama administration uses to describe these attacks.

The news media, of course, rejects these charges, and vigorously defends its reporting as balanced, objective and fair, insisting that it is merely doing its job by asking politicians 'tough' questions. Back in Thomas Jefferson's day, the press was unreservedly partisan, and un-restrained in hurling invectives and diatribes against politicians and policies it opposed. Publications with opposite political allegiances matched each other's vitriol and insults in kind, and there was no pretense or false claims about objectivity. That is what distinguishes

27 http://www.forbes.com/sites/currentevents/2016/03/23/when-excess-is-a-virtue/#6f8799b034b5

28 http://www.nytimes.com/2016/07/16/world/europe/nice-france-truck-attack-what-we-know.html?_r=0

the insidious manipulations of the news today from the unashamedly partisan reports of the eighteenth and nineteenth century press, and makes it so corrosive of civil society and government: the pretense that the news is reported impartially today.

People don't want partisan journalism any more: people want journalism to be "fair, balanced, accurate, and complete".[29] They want to make up their own minds, and prefer to get their news from sources that have no political point of view.[30]

Few people believe the news media's own claims about its impartiality, fairness and balance. According to a poll conducted by the Pew Research Center in 2009, 63% of the public believed that most news reports were inaccurate, and 60% believed that news organizations were politically biased.[31] These were the lowest figures in 20 years, and applied to all news outlets: national newspapers like the *New York Times*, all three cable news outlets (CNN, MSNBC, Fox News), national broadcast TV networks and NPR.[32]

In 2016, a poll found that trust in the news had fallen to an all-time low, with only 6% of the public saying they had a lot of confidence in the media, well below the public's level of confidence in other institutions—about the level of confidence the public had in Congress. In May, 2016, a telephone and on-line Rasmussen survey

---

29 https://www.americanpressinstitute.org/publications/reports/survey-research/trust-news/

30 http://www.people-press.org/2012/02/07/section-3-perceptions-of-bias-news-knowledge/

31 http://www.people-press.org/2009/09/13/press-accuracy-rating-hits-two-decade-low/

32 http://www.pewresearch.org/subjects/media-bias/

found that 49% of likely voters believed the Media was biased against Trump but only 18% biased against Hillary Clinton.[33]

In *'How We Know What Isn't So'*, Professor Thomas Gilovich, a cognitive scientist at Cornell University, explained how people 'know' things that are simply not true.[34] Much of it has to do with the information people are exposed to, and how they are exposed to it.

People construct mental models of reality and of how the world works from the information they are exposed to, and mental models once formed are not easily changed. People will hold on to their beliefs about the world when confronted with conflicting evidence, and therein lies the danger of media bias—the false social realities it creates become accepted social facts and truths that are difficult to correct. And false social realities that are believed can have serious social costs and consequences.

---

33 http://www.rasmussenreports.com/public_content/politics/elections/election_2016/voters_see_more_anti_trump_pro_hillary_bias_in_media
34 Thomas Gilovich, How We Know What Isn't So, The Free Press, New York 1991.

CHAPTER 2

Truth Rarely Catches Up With the Lie

• • •

"No matter how big the lie is, repeated often enough
and the masses will regard it as the truth."

JOHN F. KENNEDY

FREE SPEECH IN AMERICA HAS come to mean allowing people to say things that others find offensive, on the theory that the best test of an idea is to allow it to compete with other ideas for acceptance in the 'market'. This bedrock justification for allowing people to say what they think was given by Justice Oliver Wendell Holmes in one of the most powerful dissents in all of American case law:

*"But when men have realized that time has upset many fighting faiths, they may come to believe…that **the ultimate good desired is better reached by free trade in ideas** -- that the best test of truth is the power of the thought to get itself accepted in the competition of the market…*

That, at any rate, is the theory of our Constitution. It is an experiment, as all life is an experiment. While that experiment is

*part of our system, I think that **we should be eternally vigilant
against attempts to check the expression of opinions that we
loathe…**"*[35] (boldface added).

Justice Louis Brandeis, echoed Holmes in dissent when he wrote
that the answer to pernicious ideas was *"more speech, not enforced
silence".*[36] And the principle was reiterated again by the great liberal
jurist, Supreme Court Justice William Brennan, who wrote:

> *"If there is a bedrock principle underlying the First Amendment, it
> is that the government may not prohibit the expression of an idea
> simply because society finds the idea itself offensive or disagreeable."*[37]

This is the great free-speech principle that sets America apart from
most other Western societies that prohibit what is euphemistically
referred to as 'hate speech'. It is the great principle the news media
invokes to demand the right to report the news however it sees fit—
and it is the great principle it violates when it demonizes individuals
who express opinions the news media disapproves of in an attempt to
silence them.

But the sobering reality is that the competition between 'truth'
and falsehoods often does not come out as it should—and therein lies
the danger of providing the public with misinformation and disin-
formation instead of trustworthy news. Another Justice of the U.S.
Supreme Court pointed this out more than fifty years after Holmes
wrote his soaring dissent when he wrote:

---

35 Abrams v. United States, 250 U.S. 616 (1919).
36 Whitney v. California, 274 U.S. 357 (1925).
37 Texas v. Johnson, 491 U.S. 397(1989).

"the truth rarely catches up with the lie...[and]*...an opportunity for rebuttal seldom suffices to undo the harm* [done by circulating false information in the market place]".[38]

The false narratives created by the circulation of misinformation, or enabling their circulation, can have disastrous social consequences. This is what happened in Ferguson, Missouri. That city was nearly destroyed by rioting because of the false narrative created by misinformation about the shooting of an eighteen year old, African-American teenager named Michael Brown, by a white police officer, Daren Wilson, on August 9, 2014. The news media helped circulate the misinformation and keep alive the false narrative the misinformation had created long after it became clear that the narrative was false.

The story the news media told the public was that Brown, an unarmed, 6 foot, 4 inch, 300 pound, African-American teenager— referred to as a 'gentle giant'—was about to go to college when he was shot and killed by Daren Wilson, notwithstanding that Brown had raised his hands, and had said to Wilson, *"Don't Shoot"*. Wilson even shot Brown in the back as Brown was running away after he was first non-fatally shot. The news media repeated this story throughout the day, every day, for weeks without checking the facts or speaking independently to eyewitnesses to the incident because the narrative fitted the media's biases and stereotypes of the police as racist.

'Hands Up, Don't Shoot' became the leitmotif of protesters who looted, set fire to, and destroyed much of the city of Fergusson to express their outrage at the shooting. It cemented the radical Black Lives Matter movement, and caused the city of Ferguson to go up in flames. The story was not only untrue, it was a deliberate lie.

---

38 Gertz v. Welch, 418 U.S. 323 (1973).

After the police released a video showing that, shortly before he was shot, Brown robbed a convenience store, and assaulted the shopkeeper who tried to stop Brown from leaving the store with a box of cigars he hadn't paid for, no one in the media stopped to ask if the picture the media was painting of Brown as a gentle giant was correct. They were too busy denouncing the police for 'trying to blame the victim'.

The shooting of Michael Brown became part of a national narrative that the police in this country are racist, and regularly gun down unarmed African-American teenagers without justification. President Obama helped perpetuate the myth by repeatedly denouncing the Brown shooting and others like it as racially motivated before the facts of any of the cases were known. Officer Wilson was quickly convicted in the court of public opinion by the news media, and, fearing for his life, went into hiding. President Obama went on television twice in four days to comment on the incident, and also issued a written statement that, while denouncing violence in general terms, made it clear that he was more concerned about how the police were handling the rioting:

> "[W]hen something like this happens, the local authorities — including the police — have a responsibility to be open and transparent about how they are investigating that death, and how they are protecting the people in their communities."

> "There is never an excuse for violence against police, or for those who would use this tragedy as a cover for vandalism or looting. There's also no excuse for police to use excessive force against peaceful protests, or to throw protestors in jail for lawfully exercising their First Amendment rights. And here, in the United States of

America, police should not be bullying or arresting journalists who are just trying to do their jobs and report to the American people on what they see on the ground," Obama said, as Ferguson burned.[39]

It took two months for the *Washington Post*'s first report to appear calling into question the circumstances under which Wilson shot Brown. It was based on the *St. Louis Post-Dispatch*'s account of Michael Brown's autopsy report and the statements of African-American witnesses that supported Wilson's, not Brown's account of the shooting.[40] President Obama didn't go on television to correct his prior statements or caution people from jumping too quickly to conclusions before the facts were known—presumably because he himself had repeatedly jumped to unwarranted conclusions before the facts were known.

A month later, the *New York Times* was still trying to keep the story alive by casting doubt on the motives of the St. Louis County prosecutor, Robert P. McCulloch, who presented Brown's shooting to a grand jury instead of indicting Wilson himself. The *New York Times* then criticized the grand jury for failing *"to bring any charges against a white officer who shot an unarmed black teenager in murky circumstances"*.

"In an unusual step," wrote the *New York Times*, *"Mr. McCulloch had said he would present all known witnesses and evidence and instead of recommending an indictment, as is usually the case, let the jurors decide for themselves what if any charges to bring."*

"The officer's testimony, delivered without the cross-examination of a trial in the earliest phase of the three-month inquiry, was the only

---

39 https://www.whitehouse.gov/the-press-office/2014/08/14/statement-president
40 https://www.washingtonpost.com/politics/new-evidence-supports-officers-account-of-shooting-in-ferguson/2014/10/22/cf38c7b4-5964-11e4-bd61-346aee66ba29_story.html

direct account of the fatal encounter...But the gentle questioning of Officer Wilson revealed in the transcripts, and the sharp challenges prosecutors made to witnesses whose accounts seemed to contradict his narrative, have led some to question whether the process was as objective as Mr. McCulloch claims."

That was on November 24, 2014. A week later, the *New York Times* published the address of Daren Wilson, potentially endangering his life and that of his pregnant wife. Three months later, the Department of Justice (DOJ), headed by Eric Holder, an African-American highly critical of the police, concluded that *"Wilson acted out of self-defense, and was justified in killing Brown"*. [41]

The DOJ determined that witnesses and forensic evidence confirmed Wilson's account of the incident that Brown, after preventing Wilson from getting out of his SUV,

"reached into the SUV through the open driver's window and punched and grabbed Wilson. This is corroborated by bruising on Wilson's jaw and scratches on his neck, the presence of Brown's DNA on Wilson's collar, shirt, and pants, and Wilson's DNA on Brown's palm....Autopsy results and bullet trajectory, skin from Brown's palm on the outside of the SUV door as well as Brown's DNA on the inside of the driver's side door corroborate Wilson's account that during the struggle [that ensued after Brown punched Wilson], Brown used his right hand to grab and attempt to control Wilson's gun." [42]

---

41 https://www.washingtonpost.com/news/fact-checker/wp/2015/03/19/hands-up-dont-shoot-did-not-happen-in-ferguson/; https://www.justice.gov/sites/default/files/opa/press-releases/attachments/2015/03/04/doj_report_on_shooting_of_michael_brown_1.pdf

42 https://www.justice.gov/sites/default/files/opa/press-releases/attach-ments/2015/03/04/doj_report_on_shooting_of_michael_brown_1.pdf

The DOJ report also found that Wilson didn't shoot Brown in the back, and that Brown did move towards Wilson as Wilson had said:

> *"The autopsy results confirm that Wilson did not shoot Brown in the back as he was running away because there were no entrance wounds to Brown's back...several witnesses stated that Brown appeared to pose a physical threat to Wilson as he moved towards Wilson."*[43]

But the truth never caught up with the lie. The *New York Times* never published an article stating that it was wrong about Wilson shooting Brown in cold blood, and wrong to think that McCullough failed to indict Brown because he was prejudiced. The Reverend Al Sharpton, continued to exploit the Hands Up Don't Shoot myth and never acknowledged its falsity. Nor did Hillary Clinton.

The *Hands Up Don't Shoot* myth circulated for days on end by the news media was still alive in the minds of protesters who gathered in New York City's Times Square two years later to protest the shooting of two black men by white police officers, one in New Orleans, the other in Minnesota, for they chanted '*Hands Up, Don't Shoot*'.

Hillary Clinton was still exploiting the Brown myth two years later and invited Michael Brown's mother to address the Democrat National Convention in Pennsylvania. She also consulted with the Black Lives Matter movement, and President Obama met with leaders of the Black Lives Matter movement in the White House.

Whether causally related to the news media's attacks on the police or not or the so called 'Fergusson effect', several police officers have

---

43 https://www.justice.gov/sites/default/files/opa/press-releases/attachments/2015/03/04/doj_report_on_shooting_of_michael_brown_1.pdf

been gunned down in cold blood around the country since the shooting of Michael Brown. Nine months after the shooting, six Baltimore police officers were criminally indicted without justification on a variety of charges for the death of Freddie Gray, a 25-year-old African-American heroin addict who sustained a fatal spinal cord injury in a police van as he was being transported to the police station, all the while banding his head against the side of the van, according to the testimony of another person being transported in the van—a fact the prosecution tried to suppress and withhold from the defense. Charges were finally dropped against two of the officers after an African-American judge found four of the officers not guilty in bench trials.

Violent crime has increased in several U.S. cities during the first months of 2016, after falling for several years.[44], [45] Although Trump's claim to that effect was vigorous attacked by several individuals, including President Obama, the FBI's latest annual report, indicating increases in all categories of violent crime for the first six months of 2016, has put the matter to rest.[46]

The news media used the same tactics to create false narratives about Donald Trump—circulation of information it never verified, followed by obfuscation of the truth after the circulated facts were proved untrue. What is so extraordinary and remarkable about Trump's nomination, given the durability of the Brown myth, is that the news media attempts to kill Trump's candidacy failed so completely.

---

44 http://www.washingtontimes.com/news/2016/may/15/homicides-violent-crimes-spike-in-us-cities-as-pol/

45 http://www.nytimes.com/2016/05/14/us/murder-rates-cities-fbi.html?_r=0

46 https://www.washingtonpost.com/opinions/trump-is-right-about-violent-crime-its-on-the-rise-in-major-cities/2016/08/05/3cf6b55e-5b11-11e6-9aee-8075993d73a2_story.html

CHAPTER 3

How the News Media Biases News

• • •

> "[T]he artillery of the press has been levelled against us, charged with whatsoever its licentiousness could devise or dare. These abuses of an institution so important to freedom and science are deeply to be regretted, inasmuch as they tend to lessen its usefulness and to sap its safety."

THOMAS JEFFERSON, SECOND INAUGURAL ADDRESS, 1805

TO GUARD AGAINST BEING MANIPULATED by the news media, it is important to be consciously aware of the tactics it uses to bias the news and sway public opinion. It is important to do that to keep the press and news media honest, because, as Kovach & Rosenstiel noted,

> *"The most profound questions for a democratic society is whether the media survives as a source of independent and trustworthy information or becomes a system of self-interested propaganda and of citizens consuming select information in "filter bubbles."*[47]

---

47 Kovach & Rosenstiel, supra note 9 at 11 (page 13)

Unlike in the UK, which requires all licensed broadcasters like the BBC to be impartial, there are no laws in the U.S. requiring the broadcast media to be impartial or accurate. Consequently, the reporting of political news is biased by both what is reported and how it is reported, and most of what is reported is subjective, opinionated, and judgmental, not factual.

The cable news networks, CNN, MSNBC and Fox News, have the greatest potential to bias the news, manipulate public opinion and create false beliefs in the public's mind, because most people get their news from these networks— except for those aged 18-29, who rely more on social media—and got their news from them about the 2016 presidential election.[48] These networks can bias the news much more than newspapers because they reach a much larger audience, and repeat the same information many times over.

The 24-hour news cycle created by these cable news networks now contains 178 hours of news because the same information is recycled every hour, throughout the day, every day. Other things being equal, a person hearing a message three time is more likely to find it persuasive than a person who hears the same message only once.[49] Therefore, the networks can easily implant false beliefs in the public's mind by repeating falsehoods, unless they overdo it, as they often did with Trump, and it backfires—because repeating a message five times is *less* effective than repeating it three times.

---

48 https://www.americanpressinstitute.org/publications/reports/survey-research/how-americans-get-news/

49 Cacioppo, JT & Petty, RE. Effects of message repetition and position on cognitive response, recall and persuasion. J. Pers & Soc Psychol 1979;37:97-109

The 24-hour news cycle has made news into a commodity that is in oversupply and recycled.[50] News anchors consistently mislead the public into thinking that the recycled news they are reporting is new information. For example, CNN's Wolf Blitzer, who anchors three hours of broadcasting every day during the week, prefixes almost every item of old news he re-reports with the statement, *"we have breaking news to report"*. Megyn Kelly's 9PM program on Fox News, *The Kelly* File, always begins with the word **Breaking Tonight** flashed across the screen to introduce news that has been reported several times before and that she then recycles.

Most of what is reported is not news at all but commentary, and much of it not even commentary on news but opinions about opinions and argument. What is reported as news is often information obtained from intermediaries and public relations people: it is unreliable, biased and partisan, and here is how the news media makes it so.

TELLING IT LIKE IT ISN'T

Sometimes, the news media simply makes outright false statements about what a politician has said, as it did about what Trump said at a news conference about Hillary Clinton's 'missing' emails, i.e. the emails she deleted because, she said, they were not work related but pertained to personal matters like 'yoga'. This is what Trump said:

> *"Russia, if you are listening, I hope you are able to find the 30,000 emails that are missing. I think you would be rewarded mightily by our press."*[51]

---

50 Kovach & Rosenstiel, supra note 9 at 249 (page 13)

51 http://www.nytimes.com/2016/07/28/us/politics/donald-trump-russia-clinton-emails.html?_r=0

Impartial observers realized from Trump's comment about the press that he was being sarcastic—but not the news media. The news media accused Trump of 'inviting' Russia to *"**hack** Clinton's emails"*[52] or to *"**hack** and publish Clinton's missing emails"*[53];

of 'urging' *"Russia to **hack** into Clinton's emails"*[54];

of 'asking' *"Russia to **hack** Clinton's emails"*[55]

The Huffington Post went further, and actually put words into Trump's mouth that he never uttered, claiming that he had said:

*"I hope Russia **hacked** Clinton's email servers."*[56]

NBC's Katy Tur— a young foreign correspondent based in London who NBC brought back and embedded in the Trump campaign to cover Trump—went even further. Seizing on the *New York Times*'s characterization of Trump's quip as a 'suggestion' by *"Mr. Trump... that Russia should violate United States law on his behalf"*, Tur asked, rhetorically, what Trump's invitation to Russia to '**hack**' Clinton's email meant for *'American sovereignty and national security'*:

52 http://www.politico.com/story/2016/07/trump-putin-no-relationship-226282

53 https://www.theguardian.com/us-news/2016/jul/27/donald-trump-russia-hillary-clinton-emails-dnc-hack

54 http://www.latimes.com/politics/la-na-pol-trump-russia-emails-20160727-snap-story.html

55 https://www.bostonglobe.com/news/politics/2016/07/27/donald-trump-says-democrats-using-mail-hack-total-deflection/twJOSkr4JxR9KacN9mumMM/story.html

56 http://www.huffingtonpost.com/entry/donald-trump-russia-hack_us_5798d1c8e4b02d5d5ed3b51a

Katy Tur @KatyTurNBC · Jul 27

Trump invited Russia to hack into Clinton's email server. What does that mean for American Sovereignty and national security @NBCNightlyNews

The *New York Times* declared that security experts were '*shocked*' by Trump's remark,[57] but all references to the security risk Trump's remark might have created abruptly ceased once the news media realized what it was effectively saying about Clinton's 'missing email'— that if they were about private matters like yoga, as Clinton claimed, they couldn't possibly pose a security risk, unless Clinton had lied about the emails she deleted.

Trump, of course, never said anything about 'hacking' anything because there was nothing to 'hack': Clinton's server had long been decommissioned and in the hands of the FBI by the time Trump made his sarcastic comment about Clinton's 'missing emails' at a news conference.

The news media usually makes false statements about what a politician has said less blatantly—by, euphemistically, 'mischaracterizing' what the candidate said instead of imputing to the candidate statements that are outright false. This is how Katy Tur repeatedly accused Trump of making factually false statements about what people had seen in the apartment of Syed Farook and his wife, Tashfeen Malik, the couple who killed nine people and wounded numerous others in San Bernardino, California in on December 2, 2015.

---

57 http://www.nytimes.com/2016/07/29/world/europe/russia-trump-clinton-email-hacking.html

After it was revealed that the police had found 12 pipe bombs and 'bomb-making tools' in the couple's apartment, several people came forward to report that they had seen suspicious activity at the shooters' apartment, but did not report it because they were afraid of being accused of 'profiling'.

For example, on December 5, 2015, Fox News reported that *"amid questions about how family members and others could have overlooked the stockpile of ammunition and explosives left behind in his home"*,

> *"A California woman reportedly noticed 'suspicious activity'... but did want 'profile' him...A man identified as Aaron Elswick told an ABC News affiliate that a fellow neighbor noticed 'quite a few packages' being delivered 'within a short amount of time' at a home registered to the mother of Syed Farook....Elswick said his neighbor also noticed the occupants of the home purportedly owned by Farook's mother 'doing a lot of work out in the garage' but perhaps 'didn't want to profile' Farook and his family."*[58]

After hearing this and other reports, Trump said at a campaign event in Iowa:

> *"I think his mother knew. I think anybody who walked into that apartment knew."*

Nevertheless, on multiple occasions Katy Tur tweeted and retweeted that Trump was making the baseless claim that people saw bombs in Farook's apartment but didn't report what they saw:

---

58 http://www.foxnews.com/us/2015/12/05/neighbor-to-family-san-bernardino-terrorist-couple-purportedly-saw-but-didnt.html

Katy Tur Retweeted

Sopan Deb @SopanDeb · 49m
AGAIN: Trump repeating baseless claim that people saw bombs all
over the San Bernardino shooters' apartments and didn't report them.

THE TRUTH, BUT NOT THE WHOLE TRUTH

What the news media reports about a candidate, and how it reports it, depends on whether the news media likes or dislikes,
agrees or disagrees, with the candidate and what is to be reported. 'Selective reporting' is the anodyne way to describe these
practices.

For example, the news media talked endlessly about the class
action law suits for fraud filed against the now defunct Trump
University for weeks, but never mentioned the scandal involving the Clintons in the same type of law suits and fraud allegations through their connection with Laureate International
Universities— a for-profit higher education business with annual revenues of $4 billion that paid Bill Clinton $16.5 between
2010 and 2014 to be its "honorary chancellor". During the same
period—while Hillary Clinton was Secretary of State—the State
Department funneled $55 million in grants to groups associated
with Laureate's founder.

More recently, after Hillary Clinton's non-confidential emails
were made public, it came to light that during her first year as
Secretary of State, Hillary Clinton insisted that Laureate Education
be included on the guest list for an education policy dinner hosted by
the U.S. Department of State: "It's a for-profit model that should be

represented," she wrote in an email in August, 2009. Several months later, Laureate hired Bill Clinton as its honorary chancellor.[59]

The news media's failure to report on the scandal involving the Clintons so dismayed Professor Jonathan Turley, a liberal law professor at the Washington University Law School, that he wrote an Editorial drawing attention to "*a dubious Laureate Education for-profit online college (Walden)*" that he noted had "*many of the common elements with other Clinton scandals: huge sums given to the Clintons and questions of conflicts with Hillary Clinton during her time as Secretary of State.*"[60] What was Laureate Education seeking in return for paying Bill Clinton such a large sum of money? Professor Turley asked.

"*That would seem a pretty major story but virtually no mainstream media outlet has reported it while running hundreds of stories on the Trump University scandal,*"[61] he wrote.

For-profit colleges came under scrutiny because of recruiting practices that violated state and federal laws, and also because they were profiting at the public's expense. Although only 12% of students attend for-profit colleges, 96% of them take out federal student loans, and account for 25% of all federal financial aid. The rate of default on these loans is three times the national average for those enrolled in traditional four-year colleges, for which tax payers have to pick up that tab, and the overall graduation rate is much lower (49% versus 70%). The Obama Administration has shut down several for-profits

---

59 http://www.rawstory.com/2016/03/hillarys-emails-reveal-lucrative-ties-to-for-profit-colleges/

60 https://jonathanturley.org/2016/06/08/the-clintons-university-problem-laureate-education-lawsuits-present-problem-for-clintons/

61 https://jonathanturley.org/2016/06/08/the-clintons-university-problem-laureate-education-lawsuits-present-problem-for-clintons/

universities for their questionable if not fraudulent practices, but not Laureate.

More commonly, the news media reports one-sided stories rather than no story at all, leaving out facts— or almost all the facts, if they reflect positively on Trump— that go against the slant the reporter wants to put on a story.

For example, the media widely reported the negative comments that the recently elected Muslim Mayor of London made about Trump as reflecting the opinions foreigners had of Trump, but not one of the networks reported that the preeminent British historian, Paul Johnson, had said of Trump in an article in Forbes Magazine that Trump was *"just what America needed"*.[62]

Katy Tur's comments and countless number of tweets and retweets are a treasure trove of examples of selective reporting of negative information about Trump. Throughout the primary season, Tur appeared almost daily on NBC's and MSNBC's pro-grams to report on the Trump campaign, and selectively tweeted or retweeted many times a day predominantly negative information about Trump, or information that implied something negative about him, usually that what he was saying was not true.

For example, in June, 2016, as Trump and Hillary were squaring off as the presumptive nominees of their parties, Katy Tur's posted several tweets about the plummeting world financial markets fol-lowing 'Brexit'—the UK vote to leave the European Union, which Trump had favored. The clear intents of her tweets was to imply

---

62 http://www.forbes.com/sites/currentevents/2016/03/23/when-excess-is-a-virtue/#55901b134b5f

that Trump's policies would be bad for the U.S. economy, given that a policy he favored had caused the financial markets to plummet. Three days after the Brexit vote, the markets recovered and continued to rise, with the Dow Jones Index reaching new record highs, but Katy Tur never said a word about this to her twitter followers or mentioned it on the air.

The week after the Brexit vote, Tur tweeted the results of the NBC/WSJ poll showing Clinton leading Trump by five points (46% to 41%) and the ABC/WAPO poll showing her ahead by 12 points (51% to 39%), but she never tweeted the result of the Quinnipiac poll that three days later found Clinton almost tied with Trump (42% to 40%), or the Rasmussen poll showing Trump leading Clinton by five points.

On January 26, 2016, six days before the Iowa caucuses, Trump gave a speech at Liberty University, after Jerry Falwell, Jr, President of Liberty University, endorsed Trump. It was a packed house, and Trump began his speech by asking Falwell if it was true that the audience was the largest in the University's history, and Falwell confirmed that it was. Katy Tur immediately tried to undermine Trump's claim by tweeting:

"Students are required to attend or face a ten dollar fine"

But Tur omitted to mention that Senators Cruz and Sanders had also both given speeches at Liberty University *before* Trump as that would have undercut the false narrative she was trying to create before the Iowa caucuses—that Trump's statement about the size of the audience he had attracted wasn't true because students were required to attend. But if that was why Trump had such a large audience, why did he have a larger audience than Cruz or Sanders?

Tur used this tactic of reporting partial truths about Trump throughout the primaries to disparage Trump and cast him in a negative light. So, for example, when she tweeted that if elected Trump would be the most litigious president in U.S. history— a conclusion she based on a *USA Today* article—she omitted to report that Trump had won 92% of the law suits he has been involved in. When she tweeted that Trump had only donated $3,500 to Nikki Halley's gubernatorial campaign in 2104 and in 2015 to imply that Trump hadn't donated as much as he had suggested, she omitted to report that $3,500 was the maximum amount Trump was allowed by law to give to an individual candidate.

Faux Questions

The public gets a lot of its information about political candidates from the answers they give to questions from the news media at interviews and news conferences. People ask questions to get information they don't have—but not political news reporters. They already know the answers to the questions they ask politicians at news conferences, and ask them to sway public opinion, and to bring the public around to the reporter's point of view about a topic.

With disfavored candidates, the news media does this by using them as foils, and asking them questions to embarrass them, entrapping them into saying things they did not mean to say, or creating illusory contradictions between their answers to questions and what they may have said about the same subject matter on an earlier occasion. What the news media asks are often not really questions at all: they are assertions or rhetorical devices for controlling the dialogue, limiting the answers the interviewee can give or challenging the interviewee, and making points and arguments that serve the questioner's purpose or agenda. Almost every question Trump was asked by a hostile news media consisted of faux questions like these.

The most common way reporters try to embarrass politicians is by making offensive statements about them to their face under the guise of laying the foundation for a question. This is what Megyn Kelly did with her first question to Trump at the First Republican debate on August 6, 2015:

> **Kelly**: *"Mr. Trump, one of the things people love about you is you speak your mind and you don't use a politician's filter. However, that is not without its downsides, in particular, when it comes to women."*
>
> *"You've called women you don't like 'fat pigs, dogs, slobs, and disgusting animals'".*
>
> *"Your Twitter account has several disparaging comments about women's looks. You once told a contestant on Celebrity Apprentice it would be a pretty picture to see her on her knees."*

These 'foundational' assertions often morph into berating mini lectures, like the following example from a question Chris Cuomo, anchor of CNN's morning show New Day, asked Trump, that didn't even end in a specific question:

> **Cuomo**: *"We need to talk policy. We need to talk the state of play within your own party, but you have commanded a different headline that needs to be addressed. You are attacking Hillary Clinton for the sexual past and indiscretions of her husband, calling her an*

enabler. We have an independent panel of voters that are smart as heck, and most of them don't like it. What is your thinking on this line of attack?"

The following is another example from Katy Tur's interview with Trump at the beginning of the campaign that also didn't end in a specific question:

"Are you concerned, though, for the people who are working for you to put up these buildings? One of the workers told the Washington Post, do you think that we're hanging out of the eighth floor window and raping and selling drugs? We're risking our lives and health; these fumes are toxic. Do you have a reaction to that."

What was Tur asking Trump to react to? Whether he was concerned for the health and safety of the people who worked for him or whether he thought he had offended them with his comments about illegal immigration from Mexico?

This mini lecture from Fox News's Bret Baier at the First Republican debate ended in a **rhetorical question**:

"Mr. Trump, you talk a lot about how you are the person on this stage to grow the economy. I want to ask you about your business record. Trump corporations — Trump corporations, casinos and hotels, have declared bankruptcy four times over the last quarter-century. In 2011, you told Forbes Magazine this: "I've used the laws of the country to my advantage." But at the same time, financial experts involved in those bankruptcies say that lenders to your companies lost billions of dollars. Question sir, with that record, why should we trust you to run the nation's business?"

The following mini lecture from NBC's Halley Jackson ended in a **complex/compound question**:

> *"Your critics say within your own party your campaign is not organized well enough, it doesn't have the money, and it doesn't have the infrastructure in the battleground states. How do you combat that perception? What are you doing to basically reassure people in your own party that you could actually win? There's a real, deep concern about that."*

What was Jackson asking Trump? Whether his campaign was well organized, had enough money, or had an infrastructure? She obviously wasn't asking him any of those things but making a point to her audience: otherwise she would have asked,

> *"Do you feel your campaign is sufficiently well organized, and has sufficient money and infrastructure in the battleground states?"*

Jackson didn't ask a question like that because she wasn't trying to obtain information, but to influence her audience and embarrass Trump.

The other way the news media berates politicians to their face in front of an audience is to ask them **loaded questions**: these are questions that contain assertions the reporter wants the audience to accept as true. Here is an example again from Tur's interview with Trump (with the loaded questions highlighted in boldface):

> **Tur**: *"International diplomacy is a delicate thing. You have to watch what you say, and **how can anyone expect that you're going to be able to get to the White House and watch your mouth***

when you've been widely panned for these Mexico comments. How are you going to be able to hold your tongue and not piss people from other countries off."

Trump: *"Do you want to change that word? Are you allowed to use that word on television?"*

Tur: *"Not anger other countries."*

Tur looked annoyed that Trump had got the better of her by not being riled by her aggressive questioning, but she did not seem to realize how incredibly rude she had been. Even veteran reporters like CNN's Wolf Blitzer, Anderson Cooper, and John King don't seem to understand that certain questions—rhetorical, loaded, compound, argumentative questions— are improper even for reporters to ask. They made this clear by repeatedly opining that Megyn Kelly's first question to Trump at the First Republican debate was perfectly appropriate because she had quoted Trump's own words.

Wrong. After she laid a foundation with her demeaning assertions about Trump, Kelly asked the following inappropriate questions:

Kelly: *"Does that sound to you like the temperament of a man we should elect as president, and how will you answer the charge from Hillary Clinton, who was likely to be the Democratic nominee, that you are part of the war on women?"*

These are **rhetorical questions**. They weren't asked to elicit information: Kelly was asserting that she did not think Trump had the right temperament to be President, and that he was part of the war on women. Had Kelly asked,

"Why did you make statements like that about women?" or
"Have you made similar statements about men?"

the questions would have been entirely proper. But she didn't ask questions like that: she asked rhetorical questions to make a point, and to embarrass Trump, and those were improper questions whether she quoted Trump's statements accurately or not.

There is one last back up tactic reporters use when all else fails to get across to an audience a point they had wanted to make—argue with the interviewee, as Katy Tur did during her interview with Trump:

Tur: *"First question: Why are we here in New York? Why aren't we out on the campaign trail?"*

After Trump answered her question, Tur started to argue with him, asserting that Trump was not campaigning enough, in order to suggest to the audience that Trump was not a serious candidate, which is what everyone in the news media believed at the time (the beginning of the campaign):

Tur: *"You're the only candidate who didn't campaign on the 4th of July. Pretty much all the candidates were up in New Hampshire: you were not there. You've had no campaign events really this week. You have no campaign events planned for next week that we know of so far. You're not campaigning that much. **How can anyone take you seriously if you are not out there showing your face?"***

Reporters can insinuate practically anything they want with a question without running the risk of being accused of making false statements, as they could be if they asserted what their question insinuated and the insinuation was not true. This works because we all tacitly assume that a question wouldn't be asked unless there was some evidence to support the supposition the question entails—unless the question is a commonplace like *"do you have any siblings?"* Yet, hard as it is to believe, Fox News's veteran reporter, Carl Cameron, actually asked Trump at a news conference

"Can a question be an attack?"

Trump had just read out the names of the 40 plus veterans organizations that had received part of the $5.6 million Trump had raised for the veterans in January, 2016, and then lashed out at the news media for having insinuated that the Trump Organization had not disbursed the money, calling one reporter 'a sleaze', and another a 'real beauty'.

Cameron said in response that reporters were only asking the same questions Trump's Democrat opponents were asking, and then asked Trump whether a question could ever be an attack. What, one wonders, would Cameron's reaction be if someone had asked him,

"Was your wife a prostitute before you married her?"

Would he consider that a scurrilous attack or blithely answer in the negative, content that the answer would put an end to the matter?

Painting Old Words New
Words take their meaning from the words surrounding them and the context in which they are uttered. Reporters can change

the meaning of what politicians have said by pruning their statements or taking them out of context. This is how the news media changed the meaning of an obvious locker room joke Trump made at a rally in February, 2016 just before the Iowa caucuses, on hearing that a person at the rally was walking around with a bag of tomatoes to throw at Trump. The news media took what Trump said on this one occasion out of context, and repeated it on multiple occasions to create the false impression that Trump was inciting violence at his rallies: the violence was actually caused by groups the news media did not want to identify or disparage—Black Lives Matter activists, Moveon.org, Bernie Sanders supporters, and other left wing groups— because the news media supported these groups.

An example of how unscrupulous news reporters try to use part of a candidate's statement to change its meaning occurred at a news conference the day before the Second Republican debate hosted by Fox News in Des Moines, Iowa. NBC's Peter Alexander tried to impugn the sincerity of Trump's current pro-life position at the news conference by challenging him with part of what Trump had told NBC's Tim Russert in a 1999 interview.

Alexander started his question to Trump with the following assertion:

Alexander: *"A group of national Iowa prolife leaders are circulating a letter that says, "anyone but Trump". Effectively they are saying that you can't be trusted as a prolife advocate—"*

Trump: *"Well that's OK. That's their opinion. And all I can say is that as you know I am prolife—"*

Alexander cut Trump off, and challenged him with what Trump had said in the 1999 interview with Tim Russert:

Alexander: *"In 1999 you said you were prochoice—"*

Trump: *"I said…what did I say? You didn't read it. Read the full statement of what I said."*

Alexander: *"In an interview with Tim Russert—"*

Trump: *"I remember the interview, but read the whole statement."*

Alexander couldn't read out Trump's entire statement because he had taken only the part of Trump's statement that he needed to insinuate that Trump was not sincere about his present pro-life position. What Alexander omitted from Trump's 1999 interview with Tim Russert did not support the false narrative Alexander was trying to manufacture, and actually contradicted it, which is, of course, why Alexander left it out.

Russert had asked Trump at the 1999 interview whether he would support the very contentious issue of partial birth abortion. Trump replied:

"Well, I am very prochoice. **I hate the concept of abortion. I hate it. I hate everything it stands for. I cringe when I hear people debate the subject.** *But I believe in choice. I am strongly prochoice* **but I hate the concept of abortion."** (Boldface added)

Alexander purposefully omitted that Trump had repeatedly emphasized to Russert that he 'hated' the concept of abortion so he could use Trump's earlier pro-choice position to cast doubt on the sincerity of his current prolife position. Alexander was being dishonest, and it was disgraceful. He wasn't genuinely interested in finding out why Trump had changed his position on abortion: he just wanted to create a narrative regardless of whether it was true or not to impugn Trump's veracity and embarrass him. His colleagues at MSNBC like Andrea Mitchell praised Alexander for *"standing up to Trump"*, and he was rewarded by being asked to stand in for Tamron Hall's eleven o'clock newscast shortly afterwards. It is why Trump repeatedly called reporters like Alexander 'dishonest'.

CHAPTER 4

Creating Falsehoods by Checking Facts

• • •

"The truth is more important than the facts."

FRANK LLOYD WRIGHT

EVERY POLITICAL SEASON, UNSOLICITED, SELF-APPOINTED 'fact-checkers' presume to vet for the public the accuracy of what political candidates say, and award 'Pinocchios' on a scale of 1 to 4 to statements they deem to be 'factually untrue' or otherwise critique their formal speeches. It is an agenda-driven, media-invented exercise used to create news, most often falsehoods about disfavored politicians, from which favored politicians have little to fear.

For example, on January 4, 2016, Bill Clinton made his first stump speech for his wife, Hillary. His encomium included a litany of the things Hillary had accomplished even before she was elected to public office. Among these accomplishments was her 1993 Healthcare Plan—nicknamed *Hillarycare*—which Bill said failed to get 60 votes in the Senate, implying that it was defeated by filibuster.

It is true that *Hillarycare* did not get 60 votes in the Senate. But it is also true that it did not pass the Senate by a majority vote. Actually, *Hillarycare* wasn't even put to a vote in the Senate because Democrat Senate Majority Leader, George Mitchell, described the plan as "dead on arrival".[63] The Democrat icon Senator Daniel Patrick Moynihan said, "*anyone who thinks* [the Clinton health care plan] *can work in the real world as presently written isn't living in it.*"

So what Bill Clinton said was factually accurate, but the meaning he conveyed with his factually accurate statement couldn't have been further from the truth. And therein lies the fundamental flaw of this fact-checking exercise: it fails to distinguish between the facts stated, the meaning of what is communicated, and, hence, the truth or falsity of statements uttered.

MSNBC's Andrea Mitchell covered Bill Clinton's entire speech. Mitchell asked NBC's Chuck Todd, the latest moderator of *Meet the Press*, to comment on Bill Clinton's speech. Both Mitchell and Todd knew that Bill Clinton's account of why *Hillarycare* failed was untrue, yet they said nothing, and no one fact-checked Bill Clinton's account of *Hillarycare*.

Katy Tur has repeatedly said on the air, "*facts and the truth don't matter to Donald Trump*," but one wonders if she knows the difference, because she retweeted a tweet by The Guardian's Bradd Jaffy, in which Jaffy asserted (in reference to a complaint by Newt Gingrich):

'*Hard to say people are distorting your words when they're quoting you verbatim.*"

---

63 http://www.nytimes.com/1994/09/27/us/health-care-debate-overview-national-health-program-president-s-greatest-goal.html?pagewanted=all

Well, Bill Clinton said on introducing his wife at a rally, *"I wish we weren't married"*, because, he explained, he could then more easily say all the good things he wanted to say about her. It does not take much imagination to see how easily Bill Clinton's exact words, *"I wish we weren't married"* could be distorted by taking them out of context, and using them to convey a very different meaning from the one he intended to convey. A simple headline would do the trick:

"'Wish We Weren't Married', Bill Admits - Is Clinton Marriage on the Rocks?".

In as much as a society's laws represent that society's values, and truth is an absolute defense to a suit for defamation, the law of defamation is a good place to start to look to see what makes a statement true or false. The law says two noteworthy things about that.

First, literal truth is not the test of whether a statement is true or false: courts look to the GIST of what is said, and whether the gist of what is said is true or false. If the gist of what is said is true, factual inaccuracies do not make a statement false.

Second, not all statements or even factual assertions are capable of being true or false. Opinions cannot be true or false: they can be agreed or disagreed with, and they can be right or wrong if they are forecasts about future events, but they cannot be true or false. Nor can what the law calls 'puffery'—rhetorical flourishes and exaggerations—be true or false.

Nor does the truth of any story lie in the minutiae of every fact. Indeed, what differentiates a narrative from a mere account of events is precisely that to narrate events is to give them a meaning beyond the details of what is narrated, whereas to give an account of them is merely a repetition of facts: a memory exercise.[64]

A good example of the absurdities that can be created by equating truth with strict factual accuracy is MSNBC's Kate Snow's response to Trump's statement that Cruz was effectively eliminated from winning the nomination outright after Trump won the New York primary.

"That's not actually true," Snow replied. Cruz had not been mathematically eliminated from winning the race, because *"he could win if he won 98% of the remaining delegates,"* she said.

What Katie Snow said was factually accurate, but it was nonsense. Trump was leading Cruz by more than 20% in each of the five states (CT, DE, MD, PA, RI) that held primaries the week after the New York primary, and Cruz couldn't possibly win the nomination outright.

The fallacy implicit in fact-checking is that a given combination of words always has a fixed meaning that can be extracted simply by reading or hearing the words spoken. Words acquire meaning from the circumstances in which they are communicated. Meaning is also added to spoken words by their inflection (prosody), and by the facial expressions and body language of the speaker.

Some ambiguity is almost always present in what people say, either because no one puts into words everything they want to communicate or because of verbal nuances in their statements. We resolve

---

64 Marilyn Lester, supra note 19 (page 16).

ambiguities in discourse without conscious awareness by making certain assumptions, crossing the t's and dotting the i's. As the noted Harvard linguist and cognitive scientist, Steven Pinker, put it,

> *"To get information into a listener's head in a reasonable amount of time, a speaker can encode only a fraction of the message into words, and must count on the listener to fill in the rest."*[65]

Without such 'filling in', the simplest of utterances can take on a multiplicity of meanings. This is what happens when a computer, after being programmed to speak English, is presented with the simple sentence, *'time flies like an arrow'*—meaning that time proceeds as quickly as an arrow proceeds. Lacking a 'filling-in' capacity, the computer will come up with four additional and quite different meanings:

1. Measure the speed of flies in the same way that you measure the speed of an arrow;
2. Measure the speed of flies in the same way that an arrow measures the speed of an arrow;
3. Measure the speed of flies that resemble an arrow;
4. A particular type of flies, time-flies, are fond of arrows.[66]

And it will not be able to tell which one was the intended meaning.

What is true of ambiguities is just as true of misstatements of fact: during *collaborative* discourse, listeners 'fill-in' by automatically correcting factual errors in what is said, and understand the point another is trying to make even if what is said contains factual errors.

---

65 Steven Pinker, The Language Instinct, Perennial Classics, New York, 1994, p 72-73.
66 Pinker, supra note 65 at 208 (page 41).

The dispositive question about the relationship between factual error and meaning and truth is:

does the factual error change the meaning of what is said so that the statement is no longer true after the factual error is corrected?

This is the question that fact-checkers NEVER ask before declaiming a statement to be true or false.

Take, for example, the following statements in Trump's acceptance speech that CNN's fact-checkers declaimed as false:

"We all remember the images of our sailors being forced to their knees by their Iranian captors at gunpoint. This was just prior to the signing of the Iran deal, which gave back to Iran 150 billion dollars and gave us nothing—"

There was a factual error in these statements because although the Iranian deal had not been *implemented* when our sailors were captured, it had already been signed. But did the error make the statement *'false'*, as the fact-checkers claimed?

To determine whether the statement was false, one has to first determine what point Trump was trying to make—the *meaning* of his statement—and that depends on context. The context for Trump's statement about our sailors and their Iranian captors was contained in the following two sentences:

"Now let us consider the state of affairs abroad. Not only have our citizens endured domestic disaster, but they have lived through one international humiliation after another."

In other words, Trump was citing the incident involving the U.S. sailors and their Iranian captors as an example of an international humiliation we, as a nation, have had to suffer. To be sure, the statement contained a factual error, but the error did not make the statement *'false'*, because it did not change the *meaning* of what Trump said.

The statement still makes the same point after the error is corrected— we, as a nation, were humiliated by Iranian soldiers forcing our sailors to their knees at gunpoint just prior to the Iranian deal being *implemented*. The factual error didn't even make the subsidiary point Trump was making false—that the only reason Iran released our sailors was that the deal hadn't yet gone through—because the point was that the sailors were released because the deal hadn't yet gone through, not why the deal hadn't yet gone through yet.

It takes little imagination to see how easily what people say can be distorted by taking their metaphors and approximations literally, exploiting ambiguities in their statements, and inappropriately "filling-in" their utterances. This is how the news media creates false social realities about events and political candidates, and this is what the Media did to Trump's campaign manager, Corey Lewandowski.

The news media—Anderson Cooper, Wolf Blitzer, Jake Tapper, Chuck Todd, and others—called Lewandowski a liar, for saying, *"I never touched her"* in response to the allegation that he forcibly yanked a female reporter almost to the ground, which even the news media admitted never occurred. Lewandowski was using an expression to deny the allegation, not making a factual claim he intended to be taken literally. But these reporters took what Lewandowski said literally, and called him a liar because a video showed Lewandowski making physical contact with the reporter's left shoulder as he brushed past her to interject himself between her and Trump, after the reporter got so close to Trump that she actually made physical contact with Trump's right hand. (See Chapter 20 for an account of this incident).

Eenie Meenie Miney Mo— What do the Facts Really Show[67]

What the news media's fact-checkers mean by 'facts' are actually statistics, and the meaning and validity of a statistic do not reside in their numerical value, but in how they were derived. What a statistic means is always open to question, and fact-checkers exploit this to undermine the statistics cited by those they oppose ideologically by interpreting them differently, and then asserting that their interpretation is '*the* truth'.

Take, for example, the following statistic Trump cited during his acceptance speech at the Republican National Convention in Cleveland on July 18th, 2016. This was one of 25 '*key claims*' that the *Washington Post* (WAPO) fact-checkers claimed '*differ*[ed] *from reality*':

> "*The number of police officers killed in the line of duty has risen by almost 50 percent compared to this point last year.*"

The WAPO fact checkers said Trump's statistic was '*wrong*' because Trump was including assassinations of police officers, and assassinations aren't shootings '*in the line of duty*', even if the police officer was on duty when he or she was assassinated.[68] If you exclude assassinations police shootings are only up by 8%, the WAPO fact-checkers said.

CNN's fact-checkers interpreted the same 'facts' differently. They conceded that

---

67 Adapted from: Stemple R: Eenie, meenie, minie, mo . . . What do the data really show? Am J Obstet Gynecol 1982;144:745-52.

68 https://www.washingtonpost.com/news/fact-checker/wp/2016/07/22/fact-checking-donald-trumps-acceptance-speech-at-the-2016-rnc/

"If we look at just police killed by gunfire, 31 officers have been killed this year, compared with 17 killed in the first seven months of 2015. That's an 82% increase."

So the CNN fact-checkers didn't claim that the statistic Trump cited was 'wrong' as the WAPO fact-checkers had:[69] they simply disagreed that the statistic was valid, because they believed that

"using percent-increase stats for such small data sets can be misleading, and 2015 was one of the safest years for police officers in history. Regarding police officers killed by gunfire during the past decade, the annual average of deaths is about 50 per year. If police deaths continued at the current rate this year, we would expect about 56 police shooting deaths in 2016. That number is not too far from the annual average, even though fatal shootings of police are up from last year."[70]

So which fact-checkers were telling the public '*the truth*' about police shootings? And why did the CNN fact-checkers use the last 10 years for comparison: why not the last 5 years or the last 20 years? Do we get '*the* truth' by taking the average over the last 10 years, but not if we average over the last 5 years or 20 years?

What WAPO, CNN, and other news outlets are trying to pass off as 'fact-checking' are actually semantic quibbles over inexact terminology that politicians use when they try to convey to lay people a point about complex questions in simple language. Fact-checking is actually a pretext to refute political arguments, not legitimately—by relying

---

69 The 'almost 50%' value is obtained by taking 31 instead of 17 as the denominator: 14÷31=45%.

70 http://www.cnn.com/2016/07/21/politics/gop-convention-speeches-fact-check/index.html?sr=twnewday072216gop-convention-speeches-fact-check1216PMStoryLink&linkId=26824589

on the persuasive power of counter- arguments—but illegitimately, by claiming that their subjective interpretations and judgments about data are 'facts'.

Take for example Trump's assertion that

"there is no way to screen these [Syrian] refugees in order to find out who they are or where they come from."

The WAPO fact-checkers claimed that this was false because anyone wishing to enter the U.S. is subjected to a rigorous screening procedure. But Trump did not say that there was 'no way to screen' refugees' at all, as the WAPO fact-checkers claimed ["Trump… *falsely claims there's 'no way to screen' refugees*"]: he said there was 'no way to screen… *in order to find out who they are or where they come from*". He was obviously saying that there was no *effective* screening, not that would-be refugees are not subjected to any screening whatsoever.

The majority of the 25 key claims WAPO 'fact-checked' were not 'false' or even factually incorrect, but statements that the WAPO fact-checkers quibbled with semantically. For example, Trump said

"Nearly 180,000 illegal immigrants with criminal records, ordered deported from our country, are tonight roaming free to threaten peaceful citizen."

The WAPO fact-checkers said this '*sounds worse than it actually is*' because

"The actual crimes committed by this group are not documented, so Trump cannot easily claim all of these illegal immigrants are threatening."

Trump also said that

> *"America has lost nearly one third of its manufacturing jobs since 1997, following the enactment of disastrous trade deals supported by Bill and Hillary Clinton."*

The WAPO fact-checkers' complaint about this statement was not that it was false, but that Trump had picked *"the high point for manufacturing jobs"* for comparison, implying that the comparison was invalid.

Nor did they criticize as false Trump's statement that

> *"Another 14 million people have left the workforce entirely."*

On the contrary, the WAPO fact-checkers admitted that

> *"the number of people who have left the workforce has certainly increased since 2009"*.

Their complaint was that *"this is usually expressed as 'the labor participation rate', not as raw employment numbers"* and that part of the reason for the increase may be an increased rate of retirement among baby-boomers.

When they couldn't dispute the numerical value of Trump's statistics, the fact-checkers attacked them as cherry-picked or misleading. For example, the WAPO fact-checkers said Trump's statement that *"Forty-three million Americans are on food stamp"* was *cherry picked* because the number of people on food stamps had decreased from its highest value in 2013. They claimed the following statement was true, but *misleading*:

> *"The number of new illegal immigrant families who have crossed the border so far this year already exceeds the entire total from 2015. They are being released by the tens of thousands into our communities with no regard for the impact on public safety or resources."*

The WAPO fact-checkers said this statement was misleading because if minors apprehended without their families are included, the 'overall' apprehensions were higher in 2015 than in 2016.

But talk about whether a statement is 'misleading' takes us back to the distinction between facts and meaning we started with: one cannot determine if what a person has said is misleading without determining what the person was trying to say.

> *For words, like Nature, half reveal*
> *And half conceal the Soul within.*[71]

This is what fact-checkers never do—and why the entire exercise they are engaged in is so specious.

---

71 Lord Alfred Tennyson, *In Memoriam.*

PART II

Into The Meat Grinder

● ● ●

Trump Announces his Candidacy

● ● ●

TRUMP HAD FLIRTED WITH A White House bid publicly several times before, but each was dismissed as a publicity stunt. This time seemed different. In February, 2015, Trump hired staff in the states that voted early; a month later he formed a presidential exploratory committee, and delayed the production of his long-running reality show '*The Apprentice*'. Three months after that he announced his candidacy for the Republican Party's nomination for President of the United States, and said he was self-funding his campaign.

Trump took the plunge on June 16, 2015. He announced his candidacy from the Atrium of Trump Tower—a 68-story building on the East side of Fifth Avenue between 56th and 57th Streets that houses the Trump Organization and Trump's penthouse residence—a stone's throw from Central Park. The Atrium is a 5-level open, public space with many high end stores like Gucci, that has a breathtaking, 60-foot waterfall on the Eastern side of the building.

Trump made an impressive entrance to address the crowd that had gathered, descending the Atrium's escalator with his elegant wife, Melania, leading the way, the atrium's waterfall serving as a backdrop. His daughter, Ivanka, introduced him. Looking regal and speaking confidently, she described her father as having succeeded in many fields, at the highest level and on an international scale, because of his vision, his brilliance, his passion, his work-ethic, and his refusal to take 'no' for an answer. It was a moving, convincing tribute devoid of sentimentality

Trump began his speech by outlining the problems facing the United States, starting with the country's trade imbalances with China, Japan, and Mexico.

"Our country is in serious trouble," he said. *"We don't have victories anymore. We used to have victories, but we don't have them. When was the last time anybody saw us beating, let's say, China in a trade deal? They kill us. I beat China all the time. All the time."*

"When did we beat Japan at anything? They send their cars over by the millions, and what do we do? When was the last time you saw a Chevrolet in Tokyo? It doesn't exist, folks. They beat us all the time."

"When do we beat Mexico at the border? They're laughing at us, at our stupidity. And now they are beating us economically. They are not our friend, believe me. But they're killing us economically."

He went onto describe how the disastrous war in Iraq had destabilized the Middle east, and the threat posed by ISIS; what a disaster Obamacare was, and ended with a simple message that left no one in doubt why he was running for President: "To Make America Great Again".

"Now, our country needs a truly great leader, and we need a truly great leader now...And we also need a cheerleader."

"You know, when President Obama was elected, I said, 'Well, the one thing, I think he'll do well. I think he'll be a great cheerleader for the country. I think he'd be a great spirit.' He was vibrant. He was young. I really thought that he would be a great cheerleader."

"He's not a leader. That's true. But he wasn't a cheerleader. He's been a negative force. He wasn't a cheerleader; he was the opposite. We need somebody that literally will take this country and make it great again. We can do that."

"So ladies and gentlemen…I am officially running… for President of the United States, and we are going to make our country great again. It can happen. Our country has tremendous potential. We have tremendous people."

Trump outlined his platform, which focused on:

- Securing our borders, and curbing illegal immigration;
- Renegotiating trade deals to bring back jobs and end the country's trade deficits with China, Japan, and Mexico;
- Getting rid of fraud and waste in government, and reducing the $19 trillion national debt;
- Rebuilding the nation's crumbling infrastructure;
- Repealing Obamacare and replacing it with something better and less expensive;
- Saving Medicare, Medicaid and Social Security without cuts;
- Strengthening the military;
- Stopping Iran from getting nuclear weapons;
- Taking care of the veterans, who had being treated 'horribly';
- Protecting the Second Amendment; and
- Ending Common Core in education.

It was an unobjectionable platform, but Trump caused an outrage with his proposals for immigration reform. He said he would

* Terminate President Obama's illegal executive orders on immigration;
* Build a wall on our southern border with Mexico to stop illegal immigrants and drugs from entering the country, and get Mexico to pay for the wall;
* Deport illegal immigrants, but allow those who hadn't broken any laws to come back legally.

It was not so much what he said, as the bombastic way he said it that created the firestorm that dominated the news:

"When Mexico sends its people, they're not sending their best. They're not sending you. They're not sending you," Trump said pointing around at his audience.

"They're sending people that have lots of problems, and they're bringing those problems with them. They're bringing drugs. They're bringing crime. They're rapists. And some, I assume, are good people.

"But I speak to border guards and they tell us what we're getting. And it only makes common sense. It only makes common sense. They're sending us not the right people."

"It's coming from more than Mexico. It's coming from all over South and Latin America, and it's coming probably— probably— from the Middle East. But we don't know. Because we have no

protection and we have no competence, we don't know what's happening. And it's got to stop and it's got to stop fast."

The reaction was fast and furious. Trump and his proposals were denounced by the news media, his opponents, and politicians of every stripe as racists, anti-immigrant, un-American, and as trading on people's fear and anger. Macy's and some of Trump's other corporate partners such as NBC, Univision, Grupo Televisa, Ora TV, and NASCAR, immediately cut their association with Trump. Washington Post's fact-checker, Michelle Yee Hee Lee, gave Trump four Pinocchios for saying that illegal immigrants were "bringing crime" across the border from Mexico. According to Lee,

"Trump's repeated statements about immigrants and crime underscore a common public perception that crime is correlated with immigration, especially illegal immigration. But that is a misperception; no solid data support it, and the data that do exist negate it."[72]

In 2012, the Republican Party's nominee for President, Mitt Romney, won only 27% of the Hispanic vote because he had proposed self-deportation as the solution to the country's illegal immigrant problem. Ever since then, the Republican Party had been trying to repair its image and relationship with the Hispanic community, and now Trump was calling all Mexicans rapists. He hadn't, of course, but perception became reality.

Far from calling all Mexican or all immigrants racist, Trump repeatedly stressed in the interviews that followed his speech that he employed thousands of Mexicans, and loved Mexicans because they

---

72 http://www.americanthinker.com/articles/2015/07/illegal_aliens_murder_at_a_much_higher_rate-than_us_citizens_do.html#ixzz49hnqnhV8

were hard working and devoted to their families. He also said re-peatedly that the wall would have a *'big door in the middle'*, and that he wanted people to come into the country but hey had to come legally.

> *"Either we have a country or we don't, and if you don't have bor-ders, you don't have a country,"* he said.

Trump had also said that illegal immigrants would be deported *"hu-manely"*, and that those who had not committed any crimes could return perhaps on an expedited basis, but what Trump actually said didn't seem to matter.

The news media and Trump's opponents spoke only of *"round-ing people up"* and *"dragging people out of their homes"* when referring to Trump's proposal to deport illegal immigrants, as if deportation had to mean using ruthless, totalitarian tactics. No one bothered to ask Trump how he actually planned to deport illegal immigrants or condemn Cruz, whose immigration proposals were much harsher in that Cruz would not allow law-abiding, undocumented immigrants who had been deported to return to the U.S.

Despite the relentless personal attacks on him by opponents and the news media, Trump did not back down, and attracted huge crowds to his rallies at which he repeated his immigration propos-als and the rationale for them, and responded to the harsh criti-cisms levelled against him. Trump towered above his rivals with his self-assurance and force of personality, and made their epithets for him like *"bully"* and *"insulter-in-chief"* sound weak and ineffective. Trump proved himself to be a shrewd judge of character and able to take the measure of a man. He used this ability with great effect against his rivals, and his attacks on them always seemed to ring true, and not the gratuitous personal insults the news media tried to make them out to be.

Trump used his ability to take the measure of a man with devastating effect against Jeb Bush, the front runner from the start. Within about a month, Trump destroyed Bush's standing in the polls from which Bush never recovered despite a war chest of over $140 million, an army of endorsements from the Republican establishment, and multiple attempts to rebrand himself.

Trump repeatedly called Jeb Bush "low energy", which fit Bush's body language to a tee. Every time Jeb shrugged his shoulders while speaking to emphasize a point, one couldn't help be reminded of what Maggie Thatcher said to his father on the eve of the first Gulf War:

"This is no time to go wobbly, George".[73]

Eventually Bush removed his glasses in an attempt to look more energetic, but he only made himself look more ridiculous.

Trump also attacked Bush's stance on Common Core, and his statements about the Iraq War and about illegal immigrants acting out of love when they broke the law.

"Just like the simple question asked of Jeb on Iraq, where it took him five days and multiple answers to get it right, he doesn't understand anything about the border or border security. In fact, Jeb believes illegal immigrants who break our laws when they cross our border come 'out of love'," Trump commented

---

73 http://www.margaretthatcher.org/archive/us-bush.asp

Trump's immigration proposals continued to dominate public discussion of the election, and the general consensus was that whatever chance Trump ever had of winning the Republican Party's nomination, he had blown it with his comments about Mexicans and immigrants. Then all of a sudden, Trump's critics were silenced.

Attacks on Trump's proposals ceased for a while after a beautiful young woman, Katie Steinle, was murdered while she was strolling on the San Francisco pier by an illegal immigrant, Francisco Sanchez. Sanchez had been convicted of a felony seven times and deported from the U.S. five times, but he had returned to the U.S. each time he was deported. Sanchez was given immunity from deportation in the "sanctuary" city of San Francisco after his latest release from prison.

Sanchez admitted to murdering Steinle. He was, in Rush Limbaugh's words *"exactly the kind of guy Donald Trump was talking about,"* and legitimized Trump's stance on illegal immigration in the eyes of many.

CHAPTER 6

Trump versus a War Hero

• • •

THE ATTACKS ON TRUMP'S IMMIGRATION proposals resumed after he appeared with Maricopa county sheriff Joe Arpaio before a crowd of 15,000 people at a rally in Arizona on July 10, 2015. Six days later, a *New York Times* article quoted Senator John McCain of Arizona as having criticizing Trump for "*firing up the crazies*" at the Arizona rally. Trump responded with a tweet in which he called McCain a '*dummy*' who had graduated last in his class in Annapolis—a claim the news media was quick to denounce as false: McCain had graduated 894th out of 899, not last, the fact-checkers pointed out.

Two days after his tweet, Trump caused a firestorm by the comments he made about Senator McCain in an interview with Republican pollster, Frank Luntz. The interview took place at the Family Leadership Summit in Ames, Iowa, and they were talking about political correctness when Luntz asked Trump whether he hadn't gone too far by calling McCain a "dummy".

Trump explained to Luntz that he was offended by McCain calling people at his rally "crazies", because he had supported McCain and had raised $1 million for his campaign.

"I liked him," Trump said. *"Not so much now because he lost, and I don't like losers."*

"He's a war hero. He's a war hero." Luntz shot back, and all hell broke loose after the exchange that followed.

Trump: *"He's a war hero because he was captured. I like people that weren't captured. So he's a war hero ..."*

Luntz: *"Do you agree with that?"*

Trump: *"He's a war hero, because he was captured, okay? I believe, perhaps, he's a war hero. But right now he said some very bad things about a lot of people. So what I said is John McCain, I disagree with him, that these people aren't crazy."*

Pundits and the Media were aghast. All Trump was really trying to say was that whether McCain was a war hero or not, he'd said some bad things about people that McCain shouldn't have said. But that was not the story the Media reported. What the Media reported was that Trump had said that McCain was *not* a war hero because he was captured. High ranking military personnel who had been imprisoned with McCain in Vietnam condemned Trump and expressed utter contempt for him in public.

Lindsey Graham, a close friend of Senator McCain, was the first of Trump's opponents to respond to Trump's statements about McCain, and called Trump "the world's biggest Jackass" during an interview, saying *"he's crossed the line with the American people"* and predicted that this was *"the beginning of the end with Donald Trump."*

Trump responded to being called a 'jackass' by Graham during a speech to supporters in Bluffton, South Carolina, Graham's home state. He called Graham an *'idiot'* and a *'total lightweight'*, and recounted how Graham had called him several years earlier to ask Trump to put a good word in for Graham with Fox & Friends, and to contribute to Graham's campaign.

> *"Today I got called a 'jackass' by this guy. And I remembered… didn't this guy call me? Four years ago, three or four years ago. Lindsey Graham, I didn't even know who he was. He said, 'Mr. Trump? This is Senator Lindsey Graham, I'm wondering if it would be possible for you to call…' and he wanted to know whether or not I would give him a good reference on Fox & Friends… and of course he wanted to know if he could come see me for some campaign contributions.….So Lindsey Graham says to me, 'please whatever you can do.'"*

> *"What is this guy, a beggar? He's like begging me to help him get on Fox & Friends. So I say okay. I'll mention your name… And he gave me his number. And I found the card!"*

Trump proceeded to read out Graham's cell phone number to his audience to prove what he was saying, and urged them to call Graham.

> *"Give it a shot,"* Trump said, *"He won't fix anything, but at least he'll talk to you."*

In the same speech, Trump mocked Rick Perry, the former governor of Texas, who had also harshly criticized Trump's comments about McCain.

> *"He put on glasses so people think he's smart. But it just doesn't work. People can see through the glasses,"* Trump said.

"So he's got the glasses, the whole deal…But he's really vicious. He used to be a nice guy. He used to see me for contributions and support. All of a sudden he wants to be a tough guy."

Perry responded by savaging Trump in a speech in Washington, D.C. to a SuperPac that was supporting Perry, saying that Trump was *"born into privilege [and] couldn't have endured for five minutes what John McCain endured for five-and-a-half years."* In his grandiloquent speech, Perry called Trump *"a toxic mix of demagoguery, mean-spiritedness and nonsense… a cancer on conservatism [that] must be clearly diagnosed, excised, and discarded,"* and, echoing the attacks on Senator Joe McCarthy half a century before, he asked *"Have you no shame, Sir?"*

Every pundit and political commentator agreed that this time Trump had gone too far: questioning McCain's heroism would surely sink his campaign. But the *Washington Post*'s headline the next day was:

"Trump Surges to Big Lead in GOP Presidential Race."[74]

It was based on a Washington Post-ABC poll, which had Trump leading with 24% of the vote, and Governor Walker second with 13%. Perry's poll numbers were so low it was doubtful he would make it onto the main stage at the first Republican debate, which only had room for ten candidates.

---

74 https://www.washingtonpost.com/politics/poll-trump-surges-to-big-lead-in-gop-presidential-race/2015/07/20/efd2e0d0-2ef8-11e5-8f36-18d1d501920d_story.html

CHAPTER 7

Trump versus a Female Reporter

• • •

THE FUROR TRUMP HAD CREATED catapulted the audience of the first Republican debate hosted by Fox News on August 6, 2015 to new and unprecedented heights: twenty-four million viewers. Everyone, it seemed, wanted to see how Trump would fare in a debate.

Time summed up the challenge facing Trump at the debate:

"The reality television star and real estate magnate rocketed to the top of polls with his bombastic rhetoric. Now he has a target on his back, and a pack of struggling rivals are ready to take aim. Trump has no experience as a debater, an extremely thin skin and a taste for school-yard insults. People want provocation from him, and he will deliver. But if he comes off as a cartoonish reality show character without an ability to handle actual policy, he might find that his frontrunner status erodes. Trump knows better than anyone how to roll out a new product. Now he has to show the stuff is worth buying."[75]

Fox News was promoting Marco Rubio, and like the screaming conservative talk show host, Mark Levin, and many Republican operatives, strongly opposed Trump's candidacy. Bret Baer, anchor of Fox News's

---

75 http://time.com/3985955/republican-debate-donald-trump-jeb-bush/

six o'clock newscast, and the Moderator of the debate began by seek-ing resolution of what had been on every pundit's mind since Trump announced his candidacy: would Trump run as an Independent if he wasn't treated fairly by the Republican establishment?

"Is there anyone on stage—and can I see hands—who is unwill-ing tonight to pledge your support to the eventual nominee of the Republican party and pledge to not run an independent campaign against that person?" Baer asked the group of candidates

Trump raised his hand, and was booed by the crowd.

Megyn Kelly, one of the two other questioners assisting Baer, started the first round of questioning, and began by informing the candidates what the topic would be:

"Gentlemen, our first round of questions is on the subject of elect-ability in the general election..."

She then turned to Trump:

Kelly: *"Mr. Trump, one of the things people love about you is you speak your mind and you don't use a politician's filter. However, that is not without its downsides, in particular, when it comes to women. You've called women you don't like "fat pigs, dogs, slobs, and disgust-ing animals."*

(LAUGHTER)

Trump: *"Only Rosie O'Donnell."*

(LAUGHTER)

Kelly: *"Your Twitter account has several disparaging comments about women's looks. You once told a contestant on Celebrity Apprentice it would be a pretty picture to see her on her knees. Does that sound to you like the temperament of a man we should elect as president, and how will you answer the charge from Hillary Clinton, who was likely to be the Democratic nominee, that you are part of the war on women?"*

Trump: *"I think the big problem this country has is being politically correct.*

(APPLAUSE)

"I've been challenged by so many people, and I don't frankly have time for total political correctness. And to be honest with you, this country doesn't have time either. This country is in big trouble. We don't win anymore. We lose to China. We lose to Mexico both in trade and at the border. We lose to everybody.

And frankly, what I say, and oftentimes it's fun, it's kidding. We have a good time. What I say is what I say. And honestly Megyn, if you don't like it, I'm sorry. I've been very nice to you, although I could probably maybe not be, based on the way you have treated me. But I wouldn't do that."

(APPLAUSE)

"But you know what, we — we need strength, we need energy, we need quickness and we need brain in this country to turn it around. That, I can tell you right now."

The next day Don Lemon interviewed Trump on CNN's 9PM show *Tonight*. He asked Trump how he thought the debate went, and then broached Trump's exchange with Megyn Kelly with a loaded/leading question:

> *"Do you think…there was an agenda on the part of Fox News to target you? And if you do, why is that?"*

With his next question, Lemmon got to what he really wanted to ask Trump about: his exchange with Megyn Kelly at the debate the previous night:

> **Lemmon**: *"Well, let's talk about Megyn Kelly because you brought her up. She did push you. She pushed a lot of people, but what is it with you and Megyn Kelly?"*

> **Trump**: *"Well, I just don't respect her as a journalist. I have no respect for her. I don't think she's very good. I think she's highly overrated. But when I get out there, what am I doing? I'm not getting paid for this. I go out there and they start saying raise your arm…and so, she's, I'm out there and she…she starts asking me all sorts of ridiculous questions, and you know, you could see there was blood coming out of her eyes, and blood coming out of her wherever, but she was, in my opinion, she was off base."*

Outrage followed. The Media and Trump's opponents decried Trump for what they said was an obscene reference to Megyn Kelly's periods. Eric Erickson, a Republican operative leading the charge against Trump, said it was really pathetic that just because Trump had to take a *'tough question'* from a journalist he assumed she was having a period. Lindsey Graham called Trump's comment *'unworthy of the office he sought'*.

Trump had, of course, made no reference to Megyn Kelly's periods: he had referred to them only in the minds of his opponents and the news media, who chose to interpret the word "wherever" as a reference to Kelly's period instead of another part of her anatomy closer to her eyes, consistent with the metaphor Trump used to describe his belief that Kelly had malevolent intentions towards him, and to disbelieve Trump when he said in an later interview with Jake Tapper that he was not referring to what the news media thought he was.

> *"Only a deviant would think I was referring to what they say I was referring to…Do you think I would make a statement like that? Who'd make a statement like that? Only a sick person would make a statement like that,"* Trump told Tapper.

But no one in the news media seemed the slightest bit interested in the 'truth' of the matter, and asserted it as a fact that Trump had referred to Megyn Kelly's periods at the First Republican debate. The myth became an established fact about Trump, repeated every time someone catalogued the outrageous things Trump had said that supposedly disqualified him from ever being elected President.

Sexist, misogynist, crass and vulgar were now added to the epithets being used to denounce Trump. *"You can't insult your way to the presidency,"* became Jeb Bush's refrain about Trump.

CHAPTER 8

Candidates Exit the Race

• • •

THE POLITICAL NEWS OVER THE next three months was tame by comparison as summer turned into fall, students returned to college, and children went back to school. On September 1, 2015, Trump met with Javier Palomarez, the CEO of the Hispanic Chamber of Commerce in Trumps office in Trump Tower. Palomarez described the meeting as *'cordial'*, and Trump as *'gracious'*, and spoke of the difference between the private Trump and the Trump the public saw.

> *"It's kind of interesting, the dichotomy between the private Donald Trump and the public Donald Trump,"* Palomarez said.[76]

Although he did not endorse Trump, and said that differences between them remained, Palomarez expressed *'shock'* at how friendly the conversation was, and said he was impressed with Trump.

> *"He was not combative, he was not rude. He was a complete gentleman… He listened a lot more than he spoke. He never once interrupted me,"* Palomarez said.[77]

---

76 http://talkingpointsmemo.com/livewire/donald-trump-hispanic-chamber-commerce
77 Id.

It was a significant observation from a national Hispanic leader, given how Trump's statements about illegal Mexican immigrants had been distorted by the news media, but it got little attention, and two days later came the big announcement everyone was waiting for: Trump had signed a pledge to support whoever was the Republican nominee.

This came as a big relief. The sword of Damocles hanging over the Republican Party was the prospect of Trump running as a third-party candidate, because that would split the Republican vote and hand the election to Hillary Clinton. The RNC wanted to end the uncertainty by having each candidate running sign a pledge that he or she would support whoever the party's nominee was. Trump was at first ambivalent as he wanted to ensure that he would be treated fairly, but he eventually signed. Everyone did.

A week later, the news about the election shifted to Rick Perry who dropped out of the race on September 10, six days before the second Republican debate hosted by CNN, and then to Bobby Jindal's attack on Trump.

The conventional wisdom was that you attacked Trump at your peril because he would attack back and then your poll numbers would go down. Undeterred, and feeling he had nothing to lose given how low his poll numbers were, Louisiana's governor, Bobby Jindal, launched a ruthless personal attack on Trump just before the second Republican Party's debate.

> *"Donald Trump is not the solution,"* he said. *"Donald Trump is full of foolishness and nonsense. Donald Trump is not a serious candidate. He doesn't take policy seriously. He has no depth, no substance. He's a narcissist, he's an egomaniac. The only thing he believes in is himself. Everybody knows this is true."*

Trump tweeted in response:

"I only respond to people who register more than 1% in the polls. I never thought he had a chance and I have been proven right."

Two months later, Jindal dropped out of the race.

The second Republican Primary debate was hosted by CNN and held in the Reagan Presidential library on September 16, 2015. It was moderated by Jake Tapper, who tried to create notoriety by asking candidates to comment on statements their opponents had made. The focus was on Trump who Tapper had obviously made a target. The following loaded/leading questions give a flavor of how Tapper moderated the debate, and of the atmosphere he created:

Tapper: *Mrs. Fiorina, I want to start with you. Fellow Republican candidate, and Louisiana Governor Bobby Jindal, has suggested that your party's frontrunner, Mr. Donald Trump, would be dangerous as President. He said he wouldn't want, quote, 'such a hot head with his finger on the nuclear codes.' You, as well, have raised concerns about Mr. Trump's temperament. You've dismissed him as an entertainer. Would you feel comfortable with Donald Trump's finger on the nuclear codes?"*

Tapper: *"You didn't answer my question. Would you feel comfortable with Donald Trump's finger on the nuclear codes? It's an issue that one of your fellow candidates has raised."*

Tapper: *"Governor Bush, would you feel comfortable with Donald Trump's finger on the nuclear codes?"*

Tapper: *"In an interview last week in Rolling Stone magazine, Donald Trump said the following about you. Quote, 'Look at that*

*face. Would anyone vote for that? Can you imagine that, the face
of our next president?' Mr. Trump later said he was talking about
your persona, not your appearance. Please feel free to respond what
you think about his persona."*

Five days after that debate, at which he had given a very lack luster performance, Wisconsin's Governor Walker also dropped out of the race
with a whimper, calling on the Republican Party to unite behind a candidate who could defeat Trump. Walker had bought into the theory
that Trump had a *'high floor but a low ceiling'*, and was only leading in the
polls because so many candidates were splitting the anti-Trump vote.

This theory tacitly assumed that once a candidate dropped out of
the race all his or her votes would go to a candidate other than Trump,
but there was no evidence to support that assumption. On the contrary, the one poll in which voters were asked who they would vote for
if they could not vote for the candidate of their choice, most people
polled said their second choice would be Trump. Still, pundits like
Karl Rove insisted that Trump had a ceiling of about 25%-30% among
Republican primary voters, and could never win the nomination.

The moderators of the Third Republican Party, hosted by CNBC,
were even worse than Jake Tapper had been: everyone agreed on that,
and the following day's headlines weren't pretty:

*"CNBC Debate Moderators Face Backlash After 3rd GOP
Presidential Debate,"* was the ABC news headline.

"How CNBC lost control of its own G.O.P. debate," was Vanity
Fair's.

"Moderators lose control at third G.O.P. debate," echoed Politico.

The Republican National Committee said the network *"should be ashamed of themselves"*. Chris Christie's quip in answer to a question from John Harwood summed up the mood in the debate:

"No, John, do you want me to answer or do you want to answer? Because -- I got to tell you the truth, even in New Jersey what you're doing is called rude."

CHAPTER 9

Muslims Celebrating 9/11 in New Jersey

• • •

THE WORLD WAS THEN ROCKED on November 13, 2015 by a series of coordinated terrorist attacks on Paris in which 130 people were killed and more than two hundred severely injured. It catapulted Trump back into the lead in the polls, and his statements following the attack created another firestorm.

Trump gave a speech at the Jefferson Convention Complex in Birmingham, Alabama before a massive crowd estimated at twenty-five to thirty thousand. He told the crowd that up to that point he had been focused on trade, jobs, and Obamacare, but the conversation had changed after Paris, and it was now about ISIS and security and keeping the country safe. *"Something's going on,"* he said, *"and we have to find out what it is."*

"I don't want people from Syria coming in because we don't know who they are...We have to have surveillance of certain mosques: we had it before and we have to have it again. We have to have surveillance and we have to be vigilant."

"Hey, I watched when the World Trade Center came tumbling down. And I watched in Jersey City, New Jersey, where thousands and thousands of people were cheering as that building was coming down. Thousands of people were cheering. So there's something going on and we have to find out what it is."

The outcry was deafening. Trump was demonized by the news media for his statements about surveillance, which it claimed was prohibited by the religious freedom clause of the First Amendment. The *Washington Post* issued a fact-checker report that gave Trump's statements about Muslims celebrated on 9/11 four Pinocchios, because that never happened, the Washington Post claimed.

The *Washington Post* quoted the following exchange between Trump and ABC's George Stephanopoulos, who interviewed Trump about his comments about Muslims celebrating on 9/11 in New Jersey the day after Trump made them:

Stephanopoulos: *"You raised some eyebrows yesterday with comments you made at your latest rally. I want to show them, relating to 9/11."*

Stephanopoulos then played the portion of a video of Trump's speech for Trump in which Trump made his statement about Muslims celebrating on 9/11. The following exchange then took place:

Stephanopoulos: *"You know, the police say that didn't happen and all those rumors have been on the Internet for some time. So did you misspeak yesterday?"*

Trump: *"It did happen. I saw it."*

Stephanopoulos: *"You saw that—"*

Trump: *"It was on television. I saw it."*

Stephanopoulos: *"—with your own eyes?"*

Trump: *"George, it did happen."*

Stephanopoulos: *"Police say **it** didn't happen."*

Trump: *"**There were people** that were cheering on the other side of New Jersey, where you have large Arab populations. They were cheering as the World Trade Center came down. I know it might be not politically correct for you to talk about it, but **there were people** cheering as that building came down — as those buildings came down. And that tells you something. It was well covered at the time, George. Now, I know they don't like to talk about it, but it was well covered at the time. **There were people** over in New Jersey that were watching it, a heavy Arab population, that were cheering as the buildings came down. Not good."* (Boldface added)

Stephanopoulos: *"As I said, the police have said **it** didn't happen."*

After quoting the exchange, the *Washington Post* opined,

*"This exchange demonstrates the folly of trying to fact-check Donald Trump. Even when confronted with contrary information —'**police say it didn't happen**'— he insists that with his own eyes he saw 'thousands and thousands' of cheering Arabs in New Jersey celebrating as the World Trade Center collapsed during the Sept. 11 attacks."*[78]

---

78 https://www.washingtonpost.com/news/fact-checker/wp/2015/11/22/donald-trumps-outrageous-claim-that-thousands-of-new-jersey-muslims-celebrated-the-911-attacks/

The *Washington Post*'s statement was demonstrably false: Trump did not say, much less '*insist*' that he saw '*thousands and thousands*' of people cheering during his interview with Stephanopoulos. Trump said that '*thousands and thousands*' of Muslims were celebrating once, during his speech at a rally, and it was a rhetorical flourish he never repeated. The *Washington Post* was applying a less exacting standard of factual accuracy than it applied to Trump.

In response to the *Washington Post* article denouncing him, Trump tweeted the following report that had appeared in the *Washington Post* itself on September 8, 2001, and demanded an apology:

> "*In Jersey City, within hours of two jetliners' plowing into the World Trade Center, law enforcement authorities detained and questioned **a number of people** who were allegedly seen celebrating the attacks and holding tailgate-style parties on rooftops while they watched the devastation on the other side of the river.*" (Boldface added)

The article had been written by Serge Kovaleski and Frederick Kunkle. When questioned about the article, Kovaleski changed the subject. He obfuscated the *Washington Post*'s false assertion about there being *no celebrations in New Jersey* by focusing on Trump's reference to thousands and thousands of people celebrating on that one occasion during a rally: Kovaleski refused to acknowledge that there had in fact been celebrations on 9/11, and to correct the *Washington Post*'s false report that there had been *no* celebrations. Trump then poured oil on to the smoldering fire.

During a speech at a rally in South Carolina, Trump recounted to the crowd what the *Washington Post* had written about Trump's interview with Stephanopoulos, and read out from the 2001 *Washington Post* article he had tweeted in response to the *Washington Post* article. Trump derided the reporter for trying to disavow an article he had written, making gestures as he spoke that mimicked the body language of a coward. It turned out that the reporter had a physical disability. The news media jumped on that fact to vilify Trump for mocking a disabled reporter in public, and created yet another false social reality about him.

Trump fired back.

"Somebody at the financially failing and totally biased New York Times said that, over the years, I have met Mr. Kovaleski. Despite having one of the all-time great memories, I certainly do not remember him."

"What I do know is that after 14 years, and no retraction, this reporter tried to pull away from the tailgate party paragraph he wrote many years ago for The Washington Post. I merely mimicked what I thought would be a flustered reporter trying to get out of a statement he made long ago. If Mr. Kovaleski is handicapped, I would not know because I do not know what he looks like. If I did know, I would definitely not say anything about his appearance."

Kovaleski retorted that he had met Trump several times while covering him in the 1980s for the *Daily News*, and had been on a first name basis with him, implicitly accusing Trump of lying. Trump would have none of it. His response to the new allegation was unbowed:

"Serge Kovaleski must think a lot of himself if he thinks I remember him from decades ago -- if I ever met him at all, which I doubt

I did. He should stop using his disability to grandstand and get back to reporting for a newspaper that is rapidly going down the tubes."

Just as the Media were milking this new story for all it's worth, events intervened yet again to vindicate Trump's position on the need for vigilance to keep the country safe.

CHAPTER 10

San Bernardino and the Muslim Ban

• • •

On December 2, 2015, fourteen people were killed and twenty-two injured in an ISIS-inspired mass shooting at the Inland Regional Center, in San Bernardino, California, just outside Los Angeles, where employees of the county health department were attending a holiday event. They were killed by two radicalized Muslim Americans, Syed Farook and Tashleen Malik. Farook had ties to a group of jihadists in California who were arrested in 2012 for attempted to travel to Afghanistan to join al Qaeda; his wife, Malik, who was born in Pakistan, pledged allegiance to ISIS leader Abu Bakr al-Baghdadi on Facebook as the attack was taking place.

Farook and Malik, who were married in Saudi Arabia in 2014, had become radicalized long before the attack, and had talked to each other about Jihad and martyrdom before they were married. Malik was able to pass a K-1 visa test and enter the country on a K-1 (fiancée) visa while communicating about jihad online.

"How does it sometimes get missed?"[79] Chuck Schumer, the Senior Senator from New York asked FBI Director James Comey at a Senate oversight hearing.

"This is going to cause great consternation to the American people, where we have two people talking about jihad for a couple of years, and most Americans have the assumption we're on top of things like this," Schumer said.[80]

President Obama used the incident to renew his call for gun control: Donald Trump immediately tweeted,

"The horrible shooting that took place in San Bernardino was an absolute act of terror that many people knew about. Why didn't they report?"

Trump's response to the San Bernardino massacre was swift and uncompromising. On December 7, 2015, in a speech on the USS Yorktown, Trump read out the following proposal, which, he told his audience, he had just posted on his website:

"Donald J. Trump is calling for a total and complete shutdown of Muslims entering the United States until our country's representatives can figure out what is going on. According to Pew Research, among others, there is great hatred towards Americans by large segments of the Muslim population. Most recently, a poll from the Center for Security Policy released data showing '25% of those polled agreed that violence against Americans here in the United States is

---

79 http://www.latimes.com/local/lanow/la-me-ln-san-bernardino-shooting-live-updates-day-eight-20151209-htmlstory.html
80 Id.

justified as a part of the global jihad' and 51% of those polled, 'agreed that Muslims in America should have the choice of being governed according to Sharia.' Sharia authorizes such atrocities as murder against non-believers who won't convert, beheadings and more unthinkable acts that pose great harm to Americans, especially women."

"Where this hatred comes from and why we will have to determine. Until we are able to determine and understand this problem and the dangerous threat it poses, our country cannot be the victims of horrendous attacks by people that believe only in Jihad, and have no sense of reason or respect for human life."

The outcry against the proposed "Muslim Ban" was unprecedented in scope and ferocity. His proposal was denounced as un-American and un-constitutional, and Trump was accused of spewing more hatred by trying to ban an entire religion, and of crossing an uncrossable line of bigotry.

Almost everyone ridiculed the proposal: *"are we going to ban the King of Jordan from entering the U.S.?"* they asked rhetorically. The *Huffington Post* announced that it was no longer treating Trump's candidacy as 'entertainment', as it had *"morphed"* into *"an ugly and dangerous force in American politics"*.[81] Jeffrey Goldberg created a new narrative by tweeting,

"Donald Trump is now an actual threat to national security. He's providing Jihadists ammunition for their campaign to demonize the US."[82]

---

81 http://www.huffingtonpost.com/arianna-huffington/a-note-on-trump_b_8744476.html

82 Id.; https://www.washingtonpost.com/news/worldviews/wp/2015/12/07/how-donald-trump-may-be-helping-the-islamic-state/

Trump's opponents jumped on Goldberg's conjectural hypothesis, and used this new narrative with which to denounce Trump.

Trump's proposal was discussed every hour on every cable news network for days, and it took more than a week for the Media to acknowledge that Trump was only proposing a *temporary* ban.

A week after Trump proposed his temporary ban, CNN hosted the Fifth Republican debate. Wolf Blitzer's first question was to Trump, and it was characteristically a loaded one:

Blitzer: *"Mr. Trump, as you mentioned in your opening statement, part of your strategy is to focus in on America's borders. To keep the country safe, you say you want to temporarily ban non-American Muslims from coming to the United States; ban refugees fleeing ISIS from coming here; deport 11 million people; and wall off America's southern border. Is the best way to make America great again to isolate it from much of the rest of the world?"*

Trump: *"We are not talking about isolation. We're talking about security. We're not talking about religion. We're talking about security. Our country is out of control. People are pouring across the southern border. I will build a wall. It will be a great wall. People will not come in unless they come in legally. Drugs will not pour through that wall,"* was Trump's reply.

Blitzer then asked each of the other candidates to comment on Trump's proposal, starting with Jeb Bush:

Blitzer: *"Governor Bush, you called Mr. Trump "unhinged" when he proposed banning non-American Muslims from the United States. Why is that unhinged?"*

Bush responded by calling Trump's *"not a serious proposal"* and by describing him as a *"chaos candidate"*, who'd make a *"chaos president"*. Trump was unfazed by the attack.

Trump: *"Jeb doesn't really believe I'm unhinged. He said that very simply because he has failed in this campaign. It's been a total disaster."*

CHAPTER 11

Final Salvos Fizzle

• • •

THE MEDIA HAD ONLY ONE tale left to tell about Trump before Yuletide and the New Year. It accused Trump of making obscene comments in a speech. This one was made up by the news media out of whole cloth.

Trump was speaking about Hillary Clinton at a rally in Michigan on Monday, December 21, 2015, and her loss to Obama in 2008. Senator Lindsey Graham had just announced that he was withdrawing, just in time to have his name removed from the candidates in South Carolina primary, and avoid an embarrassing loss in his own state. Trump said"

"She was going to beat Obama. I don't know who would be worse. I don't know. How does it get worse? She was going to beat — she was favored to win, and she got schlonged. She lost, I mean she lost."

Every hourly program on every news network the next day began with the story that Trump had used obscene language to describe Hillary Clinton's defeat in 2008: he said she got *"schlonged"*. '*Schlong*' the news media told the public, was a vulgar Yiddish slang for male genitalia. Trump's vulgarity had crossed another line: it was a new low.

The furor lasted about three days. Even the distinguished linguist, Steven Pinker, entered the fray to point out that '*Goyim*' often got Yiddish expressions wrong, and that there was no such Yiddish verb as '*schlonged*'. It was unclear if the professor was intending to pour water or oil on the fire that Trump's use of the word '*schlonged*' had ignited, but matters were put to rest by the liberal Jewish political pundit, Jeff Greenfield, who admitted in a tweet, that in New York Yiddish at least '*schlonged*' meant '*badly beaten*'. On that authority the news faded from the headlines, despite attempts by the likes of CNN's Jake Tapper to keep it alive.

Hillary Clinton couldn't help herself, and characterized Trump's use of the word '*schlonged*' to describe her loss to Obama as "*a penchant for sexism*". Trump shot back:

> "*Hillary, when you complain about 'a penchant for sexism,' who are you referring to. I have great respect for women. BE CAREFUL!*"

The Trump campaign's spokesperson, Katrina Pierson, didn't mince her words.

> "*Hillary Clinton has some nerve to talk about the war on women and the bigotry toward women when she has a serious problem in her husband. I can think of quite a few women who have been bullied by Hillary Clinton to hide her husband's misogynist, sexist secrets*," Pierson told CNN's Kate Bolduan.

Pierson went on to remind viewers that while he was president Bill Clinton paid $850,000 to Paula Jones to settle a long-running sexual harassment lawsuit, admitted that he had a sexual relationship with former Arkansas state employee Gennifer Flowers, and had engaged in a tryst with White House intern Monica Lewinsky that led to his impeachment in 1998, and loss of his law license for committing perjury. Nothing further was heard about Trump's alleged '*penchant for sexism*' from the Clintons. But two more salvos were left.

Establishment Republicans made one last, desperate attempt to derail Trump's candidacy before the February 1, 2016 Iowa caucuses: National Review published a special issue with the caption, '*Conservatives Against Trump*' on its front cover. It was called a "Symposium" to which prominent conservative pundits, radio talk show hosts, and operatives contributed vitriolic denunciations of Trump, full of warnings about what would happen if Trump were to win the Republican nomination. Like all previous attempts to kill Trump's campaign, it was a complete failure.

Then on December 22, 2015, MSNBC aired, *Citizen Trump*, a documentary narrated by Chris Mathews that featured the liberal journalists Jonathan Alter and Tom Brokaw, who disparaged Trump at every possible opportunity throughout the piece. A couple of Trump supporters like Ann Coulter were allowed brief cameo appearances, but there wasn't even a pretense at a balanced treatment.

Tom Brokaw tried to diminish Trump's success in the New York real estate market by saying that '*New York real estate is about tax abatement*'. It was a fatuous comment about a treacherous market that requires developers to successfully handle City Hall, Unions, and the Mob. Jonathan Alter repeatedly asserted that Trump could not win a general election even if he won the nomination. And the narrative portrayed Trump as a thrice divorced, shallow, vulgar, philanderer, without any mention of his children's success.

CHAPTER 12

With Egg on their Faces

• • •

Jeb Bush's prediction that Trump would fade by December 15, 2015 proved to be a pipe-dream, but one that the news media and the political class shared. As late as December 8, 2015, Bill Kristol, Editor of The Weekly Standard said on Fox News that he was

"sticking with my prediction: Trump will win no caucuses or primaries, and will run behind Ron Paul in 2012 in Iowa and New Hampshire."

It was, to say the least, embarrassing, but part of a tireless effort by the news media and political class to dismiss Trump as a racist, sexist, misogynist, anti-immigrant, anti-Muslim xenophobe, who was vulgar and obscene, who referred to women's menstrual periods, mocked a disabled journalist in public, and questioned the heroism of a national hero that failed miserably to derail Trump's campaign. On the contrary, Trump broke through his putative 30% ceiling, and was on top at 35.1% in a *RealClearPolitics* average six months after he entered the race.

Political consultants, analysts, strategists, and commentators had made collective fools of themselves, but not because their predictions were so incorrect, and their attempts to dismiss Trump as a joke so misplaced. It wasn't even simply because they obviously failed to recognize that Trump was causing a paradigm shift in politics. It was because they were so arrogant that they didn't even consider the possibility that their assessment of Trump's candidacy could be wrong—despite all the evidence staring them in the face.

No one displayed their collective arrogance and incompetence more clearly than the flamboyant Mike Murphy, who has a reputation for *"aggressively hoovering every last nickel from his clients' campaigns regardless of whether he delivers a win"*, and who ran Jeb Bush's $118 million *Right to Rise* SuperPac. Murphy spent $30 million attacking Rubio, but did not use any of his war chest to try to take Trump down, declaring him a *"zombie frontrunner"* and *"other people's problem"*.

No less asinine, if more irritating, was S.E. Cupp, a millennial who co-hosted MSNBC's unsuccessful program, *The Cycle*, but is now employed as a 'commentator' by CNN. She regularly referred to Trump as *"repulsive"*, and after Trump proposed his temporary Muslim ban, leapt on to her high horse to declare:

"Frankly, I don't know how Trump surrogates can sleep at night peddling this unconstitutional, un-conservative and un-American garbage for a guy who — let's face it — will never be president."

Back in August, 2015, Cupp blamed Trump's ascendancy squarely on the political correctness of liberals:

"I have a different explanation for ascendant Trumpism," she wrote. *"It isn't the result of conservatism but of liberalism. Thanks*

to unrelenting demands by the left for increasingly preposterous levels of political correctness over the past decade, people are simply fed up. Trump survives -- nay, thrives! -- because he is seen as the antidote, bravely and unimpeachably standing athwart political correctness."

Six months later, she said to Trump supporter, Adriana Cohen, on the air:

"Political correctness has nothing to do with reality and facts... Political correctness has been used as a cudgel through this entire election to defend every asinine thing Donald Trump has said."

But so what? Only political candidates flip-flop, not political pundits. Right?

Anna Navarro, friend of Jeb Bush and Marco Rubio, who is also employed by CNN as a 'consultant', described herself as leader of the *Dump Trump* movement, and earnestly thanked Trump for attacking Bush and Rubio claiming it made Bush and Rubio *"look that much more substantial and that much more serious."*

The news media and the regular army of political operatives it invited to disparage Trump on the air spared nothing in denouncing and morally condemning Trump, and were in no frame of mind to learn anything from getting every prediction wrong, or their inability to kill the Trump candidacy. Their response to this collective failure was to search for scapegoats to blame and to redouble their efforts to bring Trump down.

Just before the New Year, former New York Governor George Pataki also dropped out of the race. *"I think the key is to stop Donald*

Trump, to not let him become the nominee before the convention," he later said. Like everyone else in the news media and the political class, he had missed that the tide of history had turned.

The Race Begins

A: February Winnows The Field

• • •

CHAPTER 13

Anything you can do Trump can do better

• • •

VOTING IN THE PRIMARIES BEGINS with four contests in February: two caucuses and two primaries, each held on separate days. They often winnow the field of candidates.

But the 2016 campaign began in earnest on January 12, 2016 with President Obama's State of the Union address. It is unprecedented for a sitting president to inject himself into primary election politics, but that is what President Obama did in his final State of the Union address. Although never mentioning him by name, in a clear reference to Donald Trump, Obama said

"rejecting any politics that targets people because of race or religion [wasn't] *a matter of political correctness… [but] a matter of understanding just what it is that makes us strong."*

"The world respects us not just for our arsenal, it respects us for our diversity and our openness and the way we respect every faith," Obama said.

"His Holiness, Pope Francis, told this body from the very spot I'm standing on tonight that 'to imitate the hatred and violence of tyrants and murderers is the best way to take their place.' When politicians insult Muslims, whether abroad, or fellow citizens, when a mosque is vandalized, or a kid is called names, that doesn't make us safer. That's not telling it what — telling it like it is, it's just wrong. It diminishes us in the eyes of the world. It makes it harder to achieve our goals. It betrays who we are as a country."

(APPLAUSE)

South Carolina's Governor Nikki Haley, who is of Indian descent, gave the Republican response, and joined Obama in attacking Trump, although also never mentioned Trump by name.

The day after Trump proposed his Muslim ban, Haley called the ban *"unconstitutional"* and *"an embarrassment"* to the GOP, and said, *"it defies everything that this country was based on. It's just wrong."* She continued her attack on Trump in her response to the President's address, saying

"During anxious times, it can be tempting to follow the siren call of the angriest voices. We must resist that temptation. No one who is willing to work hard, abide by our laws, and love our traditions should ever feel unwelcome in this country."

This inauspicious start to the year for Trump was followed three days later by the Sixth Republican debate hosted by Fox Business News in Charleston, South Carolina. As expected, Trump was asked about the comments Nikki Haley had directed at him.

Bartiromo: *"Mr. Trump, South Carolina Governor Nikki Haley in her response to the State of the Union address appeared to choose sides within the party, saying Republicans should resist, quote, 'the siren call of the angriest voices'. She confirmed, she was referring to you among others. Was she out of line? And, how would a President Trump unite the party?"*

Trump: *"Okay. First of all, Nikki this afternoon said I'm a friend of hers. Actually a close friend. And wherever you are sitting Nikki, I'm a friend. We're friends. That's good."*

(LAUGHTER)

"But she did say there was anger. And I could say, oh, I'm not angry. I'm very angry because our country is being run horribly and I will gladly accept the mantle of anger. Our military is a disaster."

(APPLAUSE)

"Our healthcare is a horror show. Obamacare, we're going to repeal it and replace it. We have no borders. Our vets are being treated horribly. Illegal immigration is beyond belief. Our country is being run by incompetent people. And yes, I am angry."

(APPLAUSE)

"And I won't be angry when we fix it, but until we fix it, I'm very, very angry. And I say that to Nikki. So when Nikki said that, I wasn't offended. She said the truth. One of your colleagues interviewed me. And said, well, she said you were angry and I said to

myself, huh, she's right. I'm not fighting that. I didn't find it offensive at all. I'm angry because our country is a mess."

(APPLAUSE)

Trump received high praise for taking hold of the issue, and not walking away from the comment. But the high point of the debate was Trump's response to the statements Cruz made about New York values.

Cruz had earlier tried to disparage Trump in the eyes of Iowans by saying at a rally that Trump embodied New York values, not Iowan values. Maria Bartiromo asked Cruz what those values were.

Bartiromo: *"Senator Cruz, you suggested that Donald Trump, quote, "embodies New York values." Could you explain what you mean by that?"*

Cruz: *"I think most people know what that means."*

Bartiromo: *"I'm from New York, I don't."*

Cruz: *"You're from New York so you might not...Everyone understands that the values in New York City are socially liberal, pro-abortion, pro-gay marriage, focus around money and the media.*

My friend Donald has taken to playing at his events, 'Born in the USA.' And I was asked what I thought of that. If he wanted to play a song, maybe he could play 'New York, New York'.

"Not too many years ago, Donald did a long interview with Tim Russert, and in that interview he explained his views on a whole

host of issues, that were very, very different from the views he's describing now. And his explanation, he said, look, I'm from New York, that's what we believe in New York. Those aren't Iowa values, but this is what we believe in New York. And so, that was his explanation. I guess I can frame it another way, not a lot of conservatives come out of Manhattan. I'm just saying."

Trump: *"So, conservatives actually do come out of Manhattan, including William F. Buckley and others, just so you understand. And just so — if I could, because he insulted a lot of people. I've had more calls on that statement that Ted made, that New York is a great place, it's got great people, it's got loving people, wonderful people. When the World Trade Center came down, I saw something that no place on earth could have handled more beautifully, more humanely than New York."*

"You had two 110-story buildings come crashing down, I saw them come down, thousands of people killed, and the cleanup started the next day, and it was the most horrific cleanup, probably in the history of doing this, and in construction, I was down there. And I've never seen anything like it. And the people in New York fought, and fought, and fought, and we saw more death and even the smell of death, nobody understood it, and it was with us for months, the smell. The air. And we rebuilt downtown Manhattan, and everybody in the world watched, and everybody in the world loved New York, and loved New Yorkers, and I have to tell you, that was a very insulting statement that Ted made."

Trump's response stole the show, and won him the debate even in the eyes of his harshest critics. But there was another debate scheduled for the following week, four days before the voting actually started. It was to be hosted by Fox News, and Trump had demanded that Megyn Kelly be removed as a moderator of the debate, because Trump believed she was biased against him, and could not treat him fairly. Fox not only refused Trump's request, but issued what even the news media agreed was an inappropriate and unprecedented press release that mocked Trump:

> *"We learned from a secret back channel that the ayatollah and Putin both intend to treat Donald Trump unfairly when they meet with him if he becomes president — a nefarious source tells us that Trump has his own secret plan to replace the cabinet with his Twitter followers to see if he should even go to those meetings."*

That of course did it. In less than 48 hours, Trump organized a fund raiser for Veterans that was held at the same time as the Fox debate, and at which Trump raised almost six million dollars. Former Arkansas Governor, Mike Huckabee, and former Pennsylvania U.S. Senator Rick Santorum joined Trump at the event following their own "undercard" debate.

CHAPTER 14

The Iowa Caucuses: February 1, 2016

• • •

HOLDING THE FOUR RACES IN February on separate days allows the candidates to greet voters one-on-one in diners and coffee shops, and to hold town hall meetings, which lets the candidates to get to know the voters and what most concerns them, and the voters see and get to know each candidate. This style of campaigning becomes impossible after February, when several states hold primaries on the same day, starting with the first Tuesday in March—called Super Tuesday because eleven states hold primaries and caucuses on that day.

The first contest of the primary season for both parties is the Iowa caucuses held on February 1st. Caucuses are antiquated, time consuming procedures, very different from primaries in which far fewer people vote. Unlike in a primary, where all people have to do to vote is show up at any time at their voting stations and cast their ballots, in order to caucus, people have to gather and register in the evening at designated caucus sites that are different from the sites where people vote in the general election, which can create confusion. Once the caucus starts, individuals called caucus captains make short speeches on behalf of their candidates, and then, to vote for a candidate, people have to congregate in physically separate areas of the room in which the caucus is held. Any candidate chosen by less than 10% of the people gathered at the caucus site is eliminated, and his or her supporters must then select another candidate, and physically go over to where that candidate's supporters are gathered and join them. The process continues until all candidates who haven't garnered sufficient support are eliminated, and then the votes are counted.

Senator Cruz was the heavy favorite to win the Iowa caucuses for two reasons. First, he was an evangelical, and a high proportion of the voters in Iowa are evangelicals. Second, he had built up a massive organization over the previous six months, referred to as the 'ground game'. His people knew where every voter was, had every voter's telephone number, and contacted each voter several times to make sure they turned up to caucus for their candidate. Trump had no ground game at all: in fact, he later admitted he didn't even know what 'ground game' meant. Never the less, one poll before the Iowa caucuses showed Trump leading Cruz by 5%, another showed him ahead by 7%.

Cruz won the Iowa caucuses by 27.6% of the vote: Trump was second with 24.3% of the vote, Rubio third with 23.1%, and Bush an embarrassing sixth with 2.8% of the vote. It was the highest primary voter turnout in Iowa history. The general consensus was that Trump had hurt his chances by skipping the Fox debate just before the caucuses. He gave a gracious concession speech, but changed his tone the following day after he learned what Cruz and his campaign had done just after the caucuses closed.

Cruz's campaign had used "dirty" tricks to advantage themselves before the caucuses even began by mailing bogus "Voter Violation" notices to voters to encourage them to turn out to vote for Cruz.

One side of the mailer read:

"ELECTION ALERT: VOTER VIOLATION" "PUBLIC RECORD" and "FURTHER ACTION NEEDED".

"VOTING VIOLATION" was printed in red on the top of the other side of the mailer, and below it an instruction to the recipient to "Read More". The recipient of the Voter Violation Notice was then told:

> *"You are receiving this election notice because of low expected voter turnout in your area. Your individual voting history as well as your neighbors' are public record. Their scores are published below, and many of them will see your score as well. CAUCUS ON MONDAY TO IMPROVE YOUR SCORE and please encourage your neighbors to caucus as well. A follow-up notice may be issued following Monday's caucuses."*

The Iowa Secretary of State blasted Cruz and his campaign for misrepresenting Iowa law to voters. Undeterred, the Cruz campaign engaged in to more dirty tricks at the caucuses, while the caucuses were still in progress.

CNN announced that Ben Carson would not be going on to New Hampshire after the Iowa caucuses, but was leaving the campaign to return to Florida, and would then attend a prayer meeting in Washington, D.C. The Cruz campaign seized on this announcement, told its caucus captains that Dr. Carson was withdrawing from the race, and instructed them to urge Carson voters at the caucuses to vote for Cruz.

What the Cruz campaign told its caucus captains and voters at the Iowa caucuses was not true: Dr. Carson hadn't decided to withdraw from the race. When Trump learned about what the Cruz campaign had done, he was furious. He accused Cruz of stealing the election, and thereafter referred to Cruz as 'Lyin' Ted'.

Rubio gave a characteristically grandiloquent speech declaring that his campaign had taken the first step at the dawn of a new American century: anyone listening to him who didn't know any better would have thought Rubio had won the caucuses, not come in third. But Rubio had exceeded expectations, and his third place finish was seen by the news media as implementing his 3:2:1 strategy: to come in third in Iowa, second in the New Hampshire primaries, and win the South Carolina primaries. Governor Mike Huckabee, and Senators Rick Santorum, and Rand Paul had performed far below their expectations, suspended their campaigns, and dropped out of the race.

CHAPTER 15

The New Hampshire Primary: February 9, 2016

• • •

SPECULATION WAS RIFE ABOUT HOW the Iowa loss would affect Trump. Would the loss let the air out of the balloon? Would his image as a winner be irreparably harmed? Would his popularity suddenly plummet? Could he recover in New Hampshire?

The polls had Trump in the lead but it was far from certain that he would win. Governor Kasich had lived in New Hampshire for several months, had held over a hundred town hall meetings in the state, and was said to be surging in the polls. Snow was forecast for voting day: would all those who came to his rallies turnout to vote for Trump? These questions were asked repeatedly every hour of every day by each cable news network.

Then came the fireworks at the Eighth Republican Debate hosted by ABCC news, two days before the New Hampshire primary. Governor Christie had made New Hampshire his fire wall, and a number of other candidates also felt it was their last chance to improve their performance, including Jeb Bush.

Bush lashed out at Trump during the debate, and attacked his use of eminent domain, but the attack back fired. Bush's brother, former President George W. Bush, had used eminent domain in Texas to obtain a baseball stadium for the Texas Rangers, of which he was once a part owner. Jeb was apparently unaware of this, and was made to look foolish and ineffectual by Trump, which played into the 'low energy' moniker to a tee.

But the real drama that riveted the audience was Christie's take down of Marco Rubio. It began with a question to Christie:

Muir: *"I do want to ask Governor Christie, Governor Christie, you said fool me once, shame on you; fool me twice, shame on me when it comes to electing a first-term senator. You heard Senator Rubio make the case that he does have the experience. Your response?"*

Christie: *"Sure. First, let's remember something. Every morning when a United States senator wakes up, they think about what kind of speech can I give or what kind of bill can I drop? Every morning, when I wake up, I think about what kind of problem do I need to solve for the people who actually elected me? It's a different experience, it's a much different experience. And the fact is, Marco, you shouldn't compare yourself to Joe Biden and you shouldn't say that that's what we're doing."*

"Here is exactly what we're doing. You have not been involved in a consequential decision where you had to be held accountable. You just simply haven't. And the fact is — the fact when you talk about the Hezbollah Sanctions Act that you list as one of your accomplishments as you just did, you weren't even there to vote for it. That's not leadership, that's truancy. And the fact is that what we need to

do — what we need to have in this country is not to make the same mistake we made eight years ago."

"The fact is it does matter when you have to make decisions and be held accountable for them. It does matter when the challenges don't come on a list on a piece of paper of what to vote yes or no every day, but when the problems come in from the people that you serve. I like Marco Rubio, and he's a smart person and a good guy, but he simply does not have the experience to be president of the United States and make these decisions. We've watched it happen, everybody—for the last seven years. The people of New Hampshire are smart. Do not make the same mistake again."

Rubio responded with impish self-confidence, unaware that Christie was about to destroy him.

Rubio: *"Well, I think the experience is not just what you did, but how it worked out. Under Chris Christie's governorship of New Jersey, they've been downgraded nine times in their credit rating. This country already has a debt problem, we don't need to add to it by electing someone who has experience at running up and destroying the credit rating of his state. But I would add this."*

It was what Rubio added that was his undoing.

"Let's dispel with this fiction that Barack Obama doesn't know what he's doing. He knows exactly what he's doing. He is trying to change this country. He wants America to become more like the rest of the world. We don't want to be like the rest of the world, we want to be the United States of America. And when I'm elected president,

this will become once again, the single greatest nation in the history of the world, not the disaster Barack Obama has imposed upon us."

Christie: *"You see everybody?"* Christie replied calmly, looking straight into the camera and at his audience.

"I want everyone at home to think about this. This is what Washington D.C. does. The drive-by shot at the beginning with incomplete and inaccurate information, and then the 25-second memorized speech that is exactly what his advisers gave him."

"See, Marco—" Christie continued, turning to Rubio and looking him in the eye.

"Marco, the thing is this. When you're President of the United States, when you're governor of a state, the 30-second memorized speech where you talk about how great America is at the end of it doesn't solve one problem for one person. They expect you to plow the snow, they expect you to get the schools open, and when the greatest natural disaster in your state's history hits your state, they expect you to rebuild your state, which is what I've done. None of that stuff happens on the floor of the United States Senate. It's a fine job, and I'm glad you ran for it, but it does not prepare you for President of the United States."

Rubio hit back, then Christie destroyed him.

Rubio: *"Chris — Chris, your state got hit by a massive snowstorm two weeks ago. You didn't even want to go back. They had to shame you into going back. And then you stayed there for 36 hours and then he left and came back to campaign. Those are the facts. Here's* *the bottom line. This notion that Barack Obama doesn't know what he's doing is just not true. He knows exactly what he's doing—"*

Christie: *"There it is!"* Christie pounced, interrupting Rubio, starring at the audience. *"There it is. The memorized 25-second speech. There it is, everybody."*

It was brutal to watch. Rubio got so flustered he repeated the same sentences, word for word, no less than five times. It was the most masterful take down of an opponent in a debate most people had ever witnessed that exposed Rubio as robotic and lacking in substance. He never recovered. But despite his masterful performance, the pundits wondered if Christie had hurt Rubio more than he had helped himself. Would Christie or his opponents be the beneficiary of his attack on Rubio? The answer was not long in coming.

Trump won New Hampshire by twenty points. Kasich was second, Cruz third, Bush fourth, which felt like victory to him. Rubio was fifth, but Christie had not helped himself by taking down Rubio. He came in sixth with 7.4% of the vote. He and Carly Fiorina suspended their campaigns, and dropped out of the race.

CHAPTER 16

The South Carolina Primary: February 20, 2016

• • •

AND THEN IT WAS ONTO the all-important South Carolina primary: Jeb Bush's fire wall. Trump was leading by double digits in the polls, but the state had a large Evangelical population which favored Senator Cruz, and Trump was facing a new barrage of attacks from his rivals and super PACs, who had spent millions flooding the airwaves with negative ads against him. In one prominent ad aired by *Our Principles* PAC, founded by a Mitt Romney aide, Katie Parker, and funded by the Ricketts family, owners of the Chicago Cubs, women read out derogatory statements Trump has made about women in the past, including Fox News anchor Megyn Kelly, and former Republican rival Carly Fiorina.

The Bushes were beloved in South Carolina, which had a large military presence, and Jeb pulled out all the stops. The super PAC supporting him spent $10.3 million on advertising in the state. His mother, Barbara Bush campaigned for him. His older brother, former President George W. Bush, who was still very popular in the State, made a stump speech for Jeb the day before the primary: it was the former President's first public appearance since leaving office. Immediately before President Bush's stump speech for his brother,

Lindsey Graham, the state's senior Senator, endorsed Jeb, calling him a friend for life whatever happened in the primary.

But it didn't all go Jeb's way in the run up to the vote. South Carolina's other U.S. Senator, Tim Scott, the only African-American in the U.S. Senate, endorsed Marco Rubio. Governor Nikki Haley, who had removed the Confederate flag from the State Capitol the previous year, endorsed Marco Rubio the day before the primary. Appearing together on the same stage for her endorsement, a governor of Indian descent, an African-American senator, and the son of Cuban immigrants, created a powerful image of diversity and unity, raising hope among Rubio's supporters that he could recover from his disastrous debate performance the previous week.

A debate, hosted by CBS, was held four days after the New Hampshire primary, a week before South Carolinians went to the polls. Following Christie's take down of Rubio at the previous debate, expectations of more fireworks were high in what was seen as Bush's last chance to salvage his candidacy. The feud between Trump and Jeb, and Trump's relentless attacks on Jeb's brother added to the electric atmosphere going into the debate, which became supercharged by heated exchanges between Trump and Bush over the Iraq war, and the reaction of the Bush lobbyists and supporters who packed the hall and booed Trump throughout the debate.

The announcement earlier in the day that Justice Scalia had passed away in his sleep while visiting a ranch in Texas, only added to the emotional intensity surrounding the debate, but the question prompted by Justice Scalia's death with which the debate began— whether President Obama should nominate someone to replace Justice Scalia, given that he only had eleven months remaining of his presidency—was not a very contentious one, and seemed to calm everyone down.

Bush seemed to realize he needed a strong performance, because he pitched into Trump the first opportunity he got, and talked over Trump to drive home his disagreement with Trump over whether the U.S. should welcome Russian's involvement in fighting ISIS:

> **Bush**: ... *This is coming from a guy who gets his foreign policy from the shows....This is a guy who thinks that Hillary Clinton is a great negotiator in Iran...This is a man who insults his way to the nomination...*

But the real fireworks started after John Dickerson, the moderator, asked Trump whether he still believed that Jeb's brother, the 43rd President, should have been impeached for lying about Iraq's alleged weapons of mass destruction in order to justify going to war with Iraq.

> **Dickerson**: *Mr. Trump...In 2008, in an interview with Wolf Blitzer talking about President George W. Bush's conduct of the war, you said you were surprised that Democratic leader Nancy Pelosi didn't try to impeach him."*

> *"You said, quote: 'which personally I think would have been a wonderful thing.' When you were asked what you meant by that and you said: 'For the war, for the war, he lied, he got us into the war with lies.' Do you still believe President Bush should have been impeached?"*

> **Trump**: *"....Obviously, the war in Iraq was a big, fat mistake. All right? Now, you can take it any way you want, and it took — it*

took Jeb Bush, if you remember at the beginning of his announce-ment, when he announced for president, it took him five days. He went back, it was a mistake, it wasn't a mistake. It took him five days before his people told him what to say, and he ultimately said, 'it was a mistake.'"

"The war in Iraq, we spent $2 trillion, thousands of lives, we don't even have it. Iran has taken over Iraq with the second-largest oil reserves in the world. Obviously, it was a mistake—"

Dickerson: So…

Trump: *"George Bush made a mistake. We can make mistakes. But that one was a beauty. We should have never been in Iraq. We have destabilized the Middle East."*

Dickerson: *"But so I'm going to — so you still think he should be impeached?"*

Trump: *"You do whatever you want. You call it whatever you want. I want to tell you. They lied. They said there were weapons of mass destruction, there were none. And they knew there were none. There were no weapons of mass destruction."*

(BOOING)

Dickerson: *"All right. OK. All right…the brother gets to respond."*

Bush: *"So here's the deal. I'm sick and tired of Barack Obama blaming my brother for all of the problems that he has had."*

(APPLAUSE)

"And, frankly, I could care less about the insults that Donald Trump gives to me. It's blood sport for him. He enjoys it. And I'm glad he's happy about it. But I am sick and tired of him going after my family. My dad is the greatest man alive in my mind."

(APPLAUSE)

"And while Donald Trump was building a reality TV show, my brother was building a security apparatus to keep us safe. And I'm proud of what he did."

(APPLAUSE)

"And he has had the gall to go after my brother."

Trump: *"The World Trade Center came down during your brother's reign, remember that."*

(BOOING)

Bush: *"He has had the gall to go after my mother. Hold on. Let me finish. He has had the gall to go after my mother—".*

Trump: *"That's not keeping us safe."*

Bush: *"Look, I won the lottery when I was born 63 years ago, looked up, and I saw my mom. My mom is the strongest woman I know."*

Trump: *"She should be running."*

Bush: *"This is not about my family or his family. This is about the South Carolina families that need someone to be a commander-in-chief that can lead. I'm that person."*

After asking Governor Kasich to comment, Dickerson turned to Rubio, who exploited the pro-Bush crowd by coming to George Bush's defense.

Rubio: *"I just want to say, at least on behalf of me and my family, I thank God all the time it was George W. Bush in the White House on 9/11 and not Al Gore."*

(APPLAUSE)

"…. George W. Bush enforced what the international community refused to do. And again, he kept us safe, and I am forever grateful to what he did for this country."

(APPLAUSE)

Trump: *"How did he keep us safe when the World Trade Center — the World — excuse me. I lost hundreds of friends. The World Trade Center came down during the reign of George Bush. He kept us safe? That is not safe. That is not safe, Marco. That is not safe."*

Rubio: *"The World Trade Center came down because Bill Clinton didn't kill Osama bin Laden when he had the chance to kill him."*

(APPLAUSE)

Trump: *"And George Bush– by the way, George Bush had the chance, also, and he didn't listen to the advice of his CIA."*

Jeb Bush obviously felt he could portray himself as energetic by being aggressive, and countering Trump's 'no energy' moniker, because he mixed it up with Governor Kasich when the debate turned to government spending. Kasich was asked about the expansion of Medicaid in his state, and gave an impressive response:

Kasich: *"...our Medicaid programs are coming in below cost estimates, and our Medicaid program in the second year grew at 2.5 percent. And Kimberly, let me tell you, when we expand Medicaid and we treat the mentally ill, then they don't live under a bridge or live in a prison, where they cost $22,500 a year. When we take the drug addicted and we treat them in hospitals, we stop the revolving door of people in and out of prisons and we save $22,500 a year."*

"Guess what else? They get their lives back. And the working poor, they're now getting health care. And you know that about a third of the people who are now getting that health care are people who are suffering very serious illnesses, particularly cancer."

"So, what I would tell you is, we've gone from an $8 billion hole to a $2 billion surplus. We've cut taxes by more than any governor in America by $5 billion. We have grown the number of jobs by 400,000 private sector jobs since I've been governor. Our credit is strong. Our pensions are strong. And frankly, we leave no one behind. Economic growth is not an end unto itself. We want everyone to rise, and we will make them personally responsible for the help that they get. And that is exactly the program we're driving in Ohio. And, boy, people ought to look at Ohio, because it has got a good formula."

(APPLAUSE)

How could anyone be so foolish as to argue with that? But Jeb Bush found a way to take issue with Kasich about expanding Medicaid:

> **Bush**: *"South Carolinians need to know this, because the Cato Institute, which grades governors based on their spending, rank him right at the bottom….South Carolinians want to make that they elect the most conservative governor or candidate that can win."*

It was a knee-jerk reaction, and it looked and sounded like it. It was difficult to escape the conclusion that Bush was just another conservative ideologue with a fixed set of proposals that he could only assert, not justify, who had nothing really to say and was arguing because that is what he felt he had to do. Kasich's rejoinder made that painfully obvious.

> **Kasich**: *"Yeah, let me say a couple of things. First of all, when Jeb was governor…his Medicaid program grew twice as fast as mine. OK? It's just a fact…You know who expanded Medicaid five times to try to help the folks and give them opportunity so that you could rise and get a job? President Ronald Reagan…"*.

Uncertainty was written on the faces of the reporters, surrogates and handlers milling around the spin room after the debate, and emotions took longer than usual to dissipate. Bush seemed energized and determined, but did he do enough? Would Trump's attack on George Bush and the crowd booing him affect his standing in the polls.

Senator Lindsey Graham was effusive in praising of Bush's debate performance:

"He had the guts to stand up to a bully," Graham said. *"This is clearly getting under Donald Trump's skin. I hope the people of South Carolina will send a message to Donald Trump that we don't like Putin, we like W."*

Glenn McCall, one of South Carolina's RNC committeeman, said in the spin room:

"I think most South Carolinians understand what President Bush did to protect our country and know that 9/11 was no fault of his, and they appreciate what he did over those eight years to respond and keep us safe."

But the GOP strategist, Curt Anderson, summed the situation up most prophetically:

"Everything we know about political strategy suggests that Trump's decision to attack George W. Bush will backfire. If it doesn't backfire, then it will be official; nothing can stop him."

"Trump's vote in South Carolina has collapsed," is how MSNBC's Chuck Todd described the findings of a WSJ-NBC poll released the day before the South Carolina primary. It was headline news: Everyone concluded that Trump's attack on George Bush had backfired, and held their breath waiting for the result.

Trump won the South Carolina primary by 32.5% of the vote, ten points ahead of Rubio, who was second with 22.5%, closely followed by Cruz in third place with 22.3%. Trump won every congressional district in the state, and collected all the state's 50 delegates. He defied expectations, and also won the Evangelical vote. Bush came in fourth with 7.8% of the vote, and dropped out of the race.

The pundits were deflated, but saw Trump's win as further proof of what they had been saying all along: Trump had a ceiling of 30%-35%, and as soon as some of the other candidates started dropping out of the race, he would start to fade in the polls.

With Bush out of the race, Rubio's second place finish in South Carolina stimulated intense speculation in the Media about Trump's chances in Florida. Trump was leading in the polls there, but everyone agreed that Rubio would likely win over most of Bush's supporters, which could put him ahead of Trump. Rubio was not expected to do well on Super Tuesday as none of the states voting that day favored him, but if Rubio won Florida, it could ignite his campaign, and catapult him into the lead of the "Establishment lane".

Three days later, on February 23, 2106 Trump went into the Nevada caucuses with a double digit lead, fresh from his double-digit win in South Carolina. Still, Rubio was expecting a strong second place finish, with a win not out of the question: he had lived in Las Vegas for six years, from the third to the eighth grade, and had his ties to the State and the Mormon community, and he had picked up the endorsements from Senator Orin Hatch, Senior Senator from neighboring Utah, and Nevada's Junior Senator Dean Heller, after Bush dropped out of the race.

Trump won the Nevada caucuses with 45.9% of the vote: Rubio came in a distant second with 23.9% of the vote, and Cruz was third with 21.4%. It was the third contest Trump had won by double digits, and the first in which he broke through his putative ceiling of 35%. Nevada also showed that Trump could win in a caucus state, which required a strong ground game. Trump won with every demographic group, including Hispanics, notwithstanding that two of his opponents, Rubio and Cruz, were sons of Cuban immigrants. Trump was beginning to look unstoppable going into Super Tuesday. Time was running out, and something had to be done if Trump was going to be stopped.

CHAPTER 17

Blitzkrieg

● ● ●

Two DAYS AFTER THE NEVADA caucuses, CNN hosted the Tenth Republican debate in Houston, Texas, four days ahead of the Super Tuesday primaries. George and Barbara Bush were in attendance. The question on everyone's mind was whether Rubio could recover from his disastrous debate performance in New Hampshire now that Christie was out of the race.

Rubio quickly answered the question in the affirmative by attacking Trump with a vengeance using facts that were not new but had never been raised before on the campaign trail. He was helped by an audience packed with millennials who screamed and whistled their approval every time Rubio answered a question or spoke not matter what he had said.

Rubio began his attack using a fine that had been imposed on the Trump organization 35-year earlier for hiring illegal Polish immigrants to work on Trump Tower. He launched his attack at the conclusion of his response to Trump's claim that Trump had made immigration an issue in the race.

Rubio: *"I also think that if you're going to claim that you're the only one that lifted this into the campaign, that you acknowledge* *that, for example, you're only person on this stage that has ever been fined for hiring people to work on your projects illegally. You hired some workers from Poland..."*

Trump: *"No, no, I'm the only one on the stage that's hired people. You haven't hired anybody."*

Rubio: *"He hired workers from Poland. And he had to pay a million dollars or so in a judgment from..."*

Trump: *"That's wrong. That's wrong. Totally wrong."*

Rubio: *"That's a fact. People can look it up. I'm sure people are Googling it right now. Look it up. 'Trump Polish workers,' you'll see a million dollars for hiring illegal workers on one of his projects. He did it."*

(APPLAUSE)

Rubio never let up. In his response to a question about the wall on the Mexican border, Rubio brought up the illegal Polish workers again, and then pivoted to the bankruptcies of Trump's casinos and the law suits involving Trump University.

Rubio: *"Yeah a couple of points. If he builds the wall the way he built Trump Towers, he'll be using illegal immigrant labor to do it. The second—"*

(APPLAUSE)

Trump: *"Such a cute sound bite."*

Rubio: *"But it -- no, it's not a sound bite. It's a fact. Again, go online and Google it. Donald Trump, Polish workers. You'll see it. The second thing, about the trade war -- I don't understand, because your ties and the clothes you make is made in Mexico and in China. So you're gonna be starting a trade war against your own ties and your own suits. "*

Trump: *"All right, you know what?"*

Rubio: *"Why don't you make them in America?"*

Trump: *"Because they devalue their currency -- they devalue their currencies..."*

Rubio: *"Well, then make them in America."*

Trump: *"Let me just tell you, they de-value their currencies. China, Mexico, everybody. Japan with the cars. They de-value their currencies to such an extent that our businesses cannot compete with them, our workers lose their jobs..."*

Rubio: *"And so you make them in China and in Russia."*

Trump: *"But you wouldn't know anything about it because you're a lousy businessman."*

Rubio: *"Well, I don't know anything about bankrupting four companies. You've bankrupted…"*

(APPLAUSE)

Rubio: *"I don't know anything about..."*

Trump: *"You know why?"*

Rubio: *"... starting a university, and that was a fake university."*

Trump: *"Here's a guy -- here's a guy that buys a house for $179,000, he sells it to a lobbyist who's probably here for $380,000 and then legislation is passed. You tell me about this guy. This is what we're going to have as president."*

Rubio: *"Here's a guy that inherited $200 million. If he hadn't inherited $200 million, you know where Donald Trump would be right now?"*

Trump: *"No, no, no."*

Rubio: *"Selling watches in..."*

(APPLAUSE)

Rubio made all that up from whole cloth. Fred Trump lent a 'small amount of money' to his son Donald to start his own business in the 1970s.[83] By the time Fred Trump died in 1999, his son had long since build his own real estate empire, and although Fred Trump's fortune has been estimated between $100-$300 million, the New York Times reported that after estate taxes $20 million was divided between Fred Trump's four surviving children.[84]

---

83 http://www.nytimes.com/1999/06/26/nyregion/fred-c-trump-postwar-master-builder-of-housing-for-middle-class-dies-at-93.html?pagewanted=2
84 http://www.nytimes.com/2016/01/03/us/politics/for-donald-trump-lessons-from-a-brothers-suffering.html

But Rubio's most vicious and successful attack concerned Trump's proposal to replace Obamacare by removing state barriers that prevent insurance companies from competing with each other in every state. Rubio mocked Trump as he repeated his answer using the refrain Christie had used against Rubio at the New Hampshire debate.

Bash: *"Mr. Trump, Senator Rubio just said that you support the individual mandate. Would you respond?"*

Trump: *"I just want to say, I agree with that 100 percent, except pre-existing conditions, I would absolutely get rid of Obamacare. We're going to have something much better, but pre-existing conditions, when I'm referring to that, and I was referring to that very strongly on the show with Anderson Cooper, I want to keep pre- existing conditions. I think we need it. I think it's a modern age. And I think we have to have it."*

(APPLAUSE)

Bash: *"OK, so let's talk about pre-existing conditions. What the insurance companies say is that the only way that they can cover people is to have a mandate requiring everybody purchase health insurance. Are they wrong?"*

Trump: *"I think they're wrong 100 percent... We have to get rid of the lines around the states so that there's serious, serious competition...You're going to see preexisting conditions and everything else be part of it, but the price will be done, and the insurance companies can pay. Right now they're making a fortune."*

(APPLAUSE)

Bash: *"But, just to be specific here, what you're saying is getting rid of the barriers between states, that is going to solve the problem..."*

Trump: *"That's going to solve the problem..."*

Rubio: *"...What is your plan? I understand the lines around the state, whatever that means. This is not a game where you draw maps..."*

Trump: *"... And, you don't know what it means..."*

Rubio: *" ... What is your plan, Mr. Trump?"*

(APPLAUSE)

Trump: *"... You get rid of the lines, it brings in competition. So, instead of having one insurance company taking care of New York, or Texas, you'll have many. They'll compete, and it'll be a beautiful thing."*

(APPLAUSE)

Rubio: *"So, that's the only part of the plan? Just the lines?"*

Trump: *"The nice part of the plan -- you'll have many different plans. You'll have competition, you'll have so many different plans."*

Rubio: *"Now he's repeating himself."*

Trump: *"No, no, no."*

(LAUGHTER) (APPLAUSE) (CHEERING)

Trump: *"... I watched him repeat himself five times four weeks ago..."*

Rubio: *"... I just watched you repeat yourself five times five seconds ago..."*

(APPLAUSE)

Everyone agreed that it was Rubio's best debate. Trump took a pounding, but even his harshest critics agreed that Trump stood up to the barrage without buckling, and showed strength.

After the debate, Rubio continued to attack Trump on the campaign trail in the build up to Super Tuesday, mocking him relentlessly with off-color schoolyard humor. Rubio looked energized, and determined to re-establish himself as the best "Establishment" candidate running

"He says I'm sweating all the time," Rubio told a cheering crowd of millennials the day before Super Tuesday, referring to Trump.

"The only reason he doesn't sweat is because his pores are blocked by the spray tan he uses. He says he is going to make America great again, but he's going to make America orange."

"Another thing he says is he's always calling me 'little Marco', and he's about six-two, which is why I don't understand why he has hands which about the size of someone who is five-two. Have you seen his hands? And you know what they say about men with small hands....they can't be trusted."

But just as Rubio thought he was getting the upper hand, Trump stole his thunder, and denied Rubio his victory lap for savaging Trump at the debate, by appearing, unannounced with Chris Christie in Fort Worth, Texas to announce Christie's endorsement of Trump. Christie continued his assault on Rubio as he endorsed Trump, thanked him for leaving the private sector when his country needed a leader, and said he, not a first term Senator who Hillary could run around the block all day, had the best chance of beating her in November. It took everyone by surprise, and shocked many seasoned Republican operatives.

Rubio continued his onslaught on Trump throughout the weekend before Super Tuesday, aided by the news media that re-aired Rubio's attacks on Trump during Thursday's debate, focusing on the law suits against Trump University. New York's attorney general, Eric Schneiderman, was interviewed several times about the law suit he filed alleging that Trump University had defrauded students with false claims. Trump responded by pointing out that Trump University had a A-rating from the Better Business Bureau, and received favorable evaluations from 98% of the students, including those who were plaintiffs in the law suits against Trump University. Trump set up a website *98%percentapproval.com* responding to Schneiderman's suite with the caption,

"You've Heard the Rhetoric, Now Learn the Truth."

CHAPTER 18

The News Media's *Faux* Racist

• • •

THE MEDIA MADE ONE LAST desperate attempt to prevent what everyone feared would be a clean sweep for Trump on Super Tuesday. On the Sunday, two days before Super Tuesday, the news media launched a new, contrived attack on Trump, and tried to make him out to be a racist. It was based on an interview with CNN's Jake Tapper. Tapper knew that Trump wasn't a racist, but concealed the evidence proving it from his audience.

Trump was in a hotel room in Florida for the interview. He couldn't see Tapper, and could only hear what Tapper was saying through an earpiece. The interview contained the following exchange about David Dukes and the KKK:

Tapper: *I want to ask you about the anti-defamation league which called on you to publicly condemn unequivocally the racism of former KKK Grand Wizard, David Duke, who recently said that voting against you at this point would be a treason to your heritage. So will you unequivocally condemn David Duke, and say you don't want his vote or that of any other White Supremacists in this election?*

Trump: *Well, just so you understand. I don't know David Duke, Okay. I don't know anything about what you're even talking about with White Supremacy or White Supremacists. So I don't know. I mean, I don't know, did he endorse me or what's going on, because you know I know nothing about David Duke, I know nothing about White Supremacists, and so you're asking me a question and I am supposed to be talking about people I know anything about.*

Tapper: *But I guess the question from the anti-defamation league is even if you don't know about their endorsement, there are these groups and individuals endorsing you, would you just say unequivocally that you condemn them and you don't want their support?*

Trump: *Well, I have to look at the group. I mean, I don't know what group you're talking about. You wouldn't want me to condemn a group I know nothing about. I have to look. If you would sent me a list of the groups, I'll do research on them, and certainly I would disavow if I thought there was something wrong. But you may have groups in there that were perfectly fine, and it would be very unfair. So give me a list of the groups and I'll let you know.*

Tapper: *Okay. I mean I'm just talking about David Duke and the Ku Klux Klan here, but ....*[85]

Tapper audibly dropped his voice, and made a face for his audience that Trump couldn't see, as he said Ku Klux Klan, and then then stopping speaking in mid-sentence. Trump, who explained afterwards that he did not hear Tapper mention the KKK, replied:

---

85 http://www.businessinsider.com/cnn-anchor-jake-tapper-donald-trump-david-duke-kkk-2016-2

Trump: *I don't know. Honestly, I don't know David Duke. I don't believe I've ever met him. I'm pretty sure I've never met him. I just don't know anything about him.*

Immediately after the interview, after he realized that Tapper had asked about the KKK, and long before the furor erupted, Trump issued a statement unequivocally denouncing the KKK. He explained that all he had heard was 'White Supremacists', and hadn't heard the question about the KKK, but his explanation was cynically derided. No one believed that he hadn't heard Tapper say 'KKK', notwithstanding that Tapper said it at the end of an incomplete sentence as he was dropping his voice.

The Media interviewed Trump's Republican and Democrat presidential opponents, as well as several lawmakers in Congress from both sides of the aisle, and asked each of them in turn to comment on Trump's alleged failure to denounce the KKK. Their response condemning Trump was aired by every cable news network every hour, every day for several days. Speculation was rife as to how Trump's ostensible failure to denounce the KKK would affect voters in the States voting on Super Tuesday, and the speculation was bolstered by the responses of voters questioned by the Media on the air. The general consensus was that Trump would be hurt by the new questions that had been raised about his views on race.

B: March Madness

• • •

CHAPTER 19

The 'Stop-Trump' Movement

• • •

DESPITE THE ATTACKS ON HIM at the Tenth Republican Party debate, and the news media's attempt to portray him as a racist, Trump won seven of the eleven races on Super Tuesday, and jumped ahead with a large lead in the delegate count. He had a very good night, but hadn't put the race away. And there was speculation that if Rubio and Cruz had attacked him earlier or there had been more time for the racist label to stick, the results might have been very different. Pundits based these speculations on Trump's narrow victory in Virginia, where Rubio was second, and won the majority of the late deciders.

Cruz won the primaries in his home state of Texas (by only 43.8%) and in the neighboring state of Oklahoma (by 6%: 34% versus 28%), and the Alaska caucuses by a thousand votes. Rubio won only the Minnesota caucuses, and was third in all but two of the remaining States. Ben Carson made a poor showing in every state, and at the end of the week suspended his campaign, and dropped out of the race.

Two days after the primaries, sensing that Trump had failed to deliver the knockout punch everyone feared he might, Trump's own party mounted a ferocious assault to try to kill his candidacy, and launched the Stop Trump movement.

Fox News was to host yet another debate—the Eleventh— two days before four states held primaries and caucuses on Saturday, March 5th, and four days before another four states held primaries and caucuses on Tuesday, March 8th. At 11:30AM on the day of the Eleventh Republican Primary debate, Mitt Romney, the 2012 Republican nominee who lost the presidential race to Barak Obama, and who lost the race for the Republican nomination to John McCain in 2008, launched the concerted effort of Conservatives in the Republican Party to prevent Trump from winning the Party's nomination with a speech he delivered at the University of Utah's Hinckley Institute of Politics in Salt Lake City.

It would be impossible to overstate the viciousness Romney's attack on Trump or his hypocrisy given what Romney had said about Trump in 2012, when Romney asked for and got Trump's endorsement.

"Being in Donald Trump's magnificent hotel and having his endorsement is a delight," Romney said back then.

"I'm so honored and pleased to have his endorsement. ... Donald Trump has shown an extraordinary ability to understand how our economy works to create jobs for the American people. He's done it here in Nevada. He's done it across the country. ... I spent my life in the private sector. Not quite as successful as this guy. But successful nonetheless."

But four years later, Romney saw fit to unleash a furious diatribe, brimming with vitriol and contempt, against the character, personality, and business acumen of the man whose endorsement he had sought so assiduously four years earlier. He delivered his speech five days before voters in the state where his father was governor,

Michigan, went to the polls. The purpose of the speech wasn't to endorse anyone, but to urge Cruz, Rubio and Kasich to stay in the race, and to ask their voters to join the attempt to Stop Trump from getting the 1237 delegates needed to win the Republican Party's nomination outright on the first ballot, and vote for the candidate most likely to win in their state—Rubio in Florida, Kasich in Ohio.

Romney started his diatribe by saying that if Republicans chose Donald Trump as their nominee *"the prospects for a safe and prosperous future are greatly diminished"*. He went on to explain why, starting with the economy:

> *"If Donald Trump's plans were ever implemented, the country would sink into a prolonged recession…His proposed 35 percent tariff-like penalties would instigate a trade war, and that would raise prices for consumers, kill our export jobs, and lead entrepreneurs and businesses of all stripes to flee America. His tax plan, in combination with his refusal to reform entitlements and honestly address spending, would balloon the deficit and debt."*

A stinging attack on Trump's business acumen and character followed:

> *"But wait, wait, wait, you say. Isn't he a great businessman? Doesn't he know what he's talking about? No he isn't, and no he doesn't. His bankruptcies have crushed small businesses and the people who work for them. He inherited his business, he didn't create it."*

The degree of dishonesty, hypocrisy and hubris exhibited by these statements from a man who had bankrupted 22% of the companies his company had invested in—three times the bankruptcy rate of companies the federal government invested in[86]—perhaps explain why Romney was so unsuccessful as a national politicians, and failed in both his attempts to run for the Presidency of the United States.

"This is a candidate who mocked a disabled reporter," Romney continued, repeating the myth the media had created,

> *"who attributed a reporter's question to her menstrual cycle, who mocked a brilliant rival, who happens to be a woman, due to her appearance, who bragged about his marital affairs, and who laces his public speeches with vulgarity…There's a dark side in his boasts about his sexual exploits during the Vietnam War, when at the same time, John McCain, whom he has mocked, was imprisoned and tortured."*

The President of the United States, and the nominees of the great political parties bore a responsibility to represent American values, Romney said, and to be an example to the world, and to our children and grandchildren, and he then asked his audience to consider

> *"Trump's personal qualities: his bullying, the greed, the showing-off, the misogyny, the third-grade theatrics."*

Romney ended his speech by calling on Trump to release his tax returns and the transcript of his interview with the New York Times, but predicted that he wouldn't because it would prove that he was a conman.

> *"Here's what I know. Donald Trump is a phony, a fraud, whose promises are as worthless as a degree from Trump University."*

---

86 http://www.truth-out.org/buzzflash/commentary/romney-s-bain-investment-record-three-times-the-bankruptcies-of-fed-investments

Romney tried to mitigate the response he anticipated to his savage attack on Trump:

> *"Watch how he responds to my speech. Will he talk about our policy differences,"* he asked fatuously, having said nothing about his own policies,

> *"or will he attack me with every imaginable low-road insult? That may tell you what you need to know about his temperament, stability, and suitability to be President."*

Romney proved himself to be as bad a judge of character as he was a good dissembler: Trump simply shrugged off his attack as "not very relevant", and explained Romney's motivation for the speech—that Trump hadn't supported Romney's plan to run for the Presidency for a third time in 2016. Trump responded to Romney's attack at a press conference a few hours after Romney gave his speech, and most of his response dealt with what Romney hadn't talked about:

> *"When he talks about me…I wrote a couple of them down…he doesn't want to talk about the Bank of America building in San Francisco or 1290 Avenue of the Americas. They don't want to talk about the West Side railroad yards where I built a city on the West Side of Manhattan, a tremendous city on the West Side. They don't want to talk about 40 Wall Street and all the buildings. They want to talk about water…which I still have…they want to talk about a magazine that I still have, and that goes to all my clubs."*

Trump explained that Trump University had a 98% approval rating, and that his opponents took down an advertisement in which two former Trump University students accuse Trump and Trump

University of fraud, because Trump tweeted a copy of the two students' evaluation forms showing that they had given Trump University high marks in every category.

Trump made Romney look foolish, and his attacks on Trump as a conman and fraud implausible, by detailing the public bid the Obama Administration put out to convert the Old Post Office building next to the White House into a hotel. Trump said that the Trump Organization won the bid because of its track record of completing projects on time and under budget, and because its financial statement was so strong that it guaranteed completion of the project.

Trump ended his response to Romney by calling Romney's wife *"a very lovely woman"*, and by conceding that Romney probably had a right to turn on him as he had opposed Romney's plan to run again in 2016. Trump didn't throw "low-road insults" as Romney had predicted, and he made Romney's attack on him appear tawdry and ineffective.

> *"So Mitt was very nasty. I thought he was a better person than that. I did help him. I raised money for him. I held two fund raisers for him...And he turned. Now I will say this: he probably had a right to turn because no one could have been more nasty than me in getting him not to run by calling him a choke artist."*

Nine hours later came the Eleventh Republican Party's debate. It was a food fight that a focus group watching the debate predicted would hurt the Republican Party. Rubio and Cruz had obviously decided ahead of time to coordinate their attack on Trump because at the first break they reached across to each other behind Trump's back to shake hands and congratulate each other.

Rubio did most of the work. He baited Trump by calling him names, and attacking him with the same themes he had used at the previous debate: the 35-year old million dollar fine for using illegal Polish immigrants to build Trump Tower; Trump's hiring of seasonal foreign workers in his Florida clubs and hotels instead of American workers; the four bankruptcies of his casinos in Atlantic City; and law suits against Trump University, calling him a 'conman'.

"He's trying to do to the American voter what he did to the people who signed up for this course," Rubio said. *"He's trying to con people into giving them their vote."*

Cruz did some attacking of his own, accusing Trump of being *"part of the corruption in Washington that* [voters were] *angry about"*—a surprising claim by a sitting Senator against someone who had never held public office— but Cruz was mostly content to sit back, watch, and when the heated exchange was over say to the moderators,

"Megyn, let me just ask the voters at home: Is this the debate you want playing out in the general election?"

The Moderators joined in the fray, and brought some homework with which to try to embarrass Trump. Mike Wallace challenged Trump's proposals to cut the deficit with statistics showing how little would be saved by eliminating the agencies Trump planned to eliminate, and by renegotiating drug prices—but he never brought estimates of how much could be saved by eliminating fraud and abuse, which was also part of Trump's plan.

It was a bruising attack that left the networks' pundits stunned and Trump's opponents beaming, but begrudgingly admitting that

Trump had, again, weathered the ferocious attacks he had been largely unprepared for surprisingly well. Everyone agreed that the results from the four states that were going to vote within 36 hours, and the other four states that were going to the polls four days later would indicate how effective the attacks on Trump had been because there was no time for Trump to reverse any negative impact those attacks may have had.

Louisiana and Kentucky held primaries, and Kansas and Maine caucuses on Saturday, March 5th. Trump and Cruz won two states each. Trump won the primaries in Louisiana and Kentucky; Cruz won the caucuses in Kansas and Maine. But Cruz had won nine more delegates than Trump, and Trump had underperformed his polling. He had been leading in Louisiana by double digits, but only won by 3%, and only because of the early votes that were cast before the recent attacks on him.

Trump's worse than expected showing in Louisiana caused many pundits to speculate that Trump may have been badly damaged by the most recent attacks on him, as everyone waited for the results from the next batch of states to vote. Romney said at an interview the next morning that he was very pleased with the result, and believed that his attack on Trump had an effect.

Trump won three of the next four contests on March 8th: each one by double digits, and two of them—Hawaii and Mississippi—with over 40% of the vote. Trump had again broken through his putative ceiling, and delivered a crushing blow to those hoping to stop him. Kasich, who had set his eyes on Michigan, and had been said to be surging in the polls, came in a disappointing third: Trump won the state's primary with 36.5% of the vote. Trump's underperformance in Louisiana proved not to be a harbingers of what was to come, and dashed the hopes of the anti-Trump movement that Trump had finally been stopped.

Winning the Mississippi primary with 47% of the vote was fairly convincing proof that attacking Trump as a racist hadn't worked, but the Trump camp had barely finished celebrating its victories before the Media launched a new attack on him, potentially much more damaging than its attempt to portray Trump a racist.

The racist moniker having failed, the news media changed tack, and exploited back to back incidents to launch a new narrative against Trump—that he was inciting violence at his rallies.

CHAPTER 20

Inciting Violence: the New anti-Trump Narrative

• • •

Trump held a press conference after the result of the Mississippi primary was announced, and an incident occurred between Trump's campaign manager, Corey Lewandowski, and a *Breitbart* reporter, Michelle Fields, just after the press conference concluded. Fields said that as she was about to ask Trump a question about affirmative action,

> *"Someone had grabbed me tightly by the arm and yanked me down. I almost fell to the ground, but was able to maintain my balance. Nonetheless, I was shaken."*

Fields made the complaint on twitter not to the Trump campaign, and never spoke with anyone from the campaign. She said she didn't see who had allegedly grabbed her arm, but the *Washington Post*'s Ben Terris identified Corey Lewandowski as the one who had "*aggressively tried to pull*" Fields to the ground. None of the other approximately hundred reporters and cameramen in the room saw what Fields and Terris were claiming occurred, and Lewandowski denied any involvement in such an incident. Trump stated that his campaign questioned the Secret Service agents who were surrounding Trump, and they said they saw nothing.

Fields posted a picture of her left forearm with a bruise on it the next day on twitter, and three days after the incident she filed criminal charges with the Jupiter Police Department.

NBC's Katy Tur posted an audio of the incident on twitter. The audio contains no yells or shouts or exclamations or any other sound one would have expected to hear from someone reacting to being suddenly grabbed by the arm and almost yanked to the ground. All that can be heard on the audio is after-the-alleged-event chatter between a few people speaking in a normal tone of voice.

The next day another incident occurred, this time in Fayetteville North Carolina, in a stadium after a Trump rally. A 78-year old man punched a protester who had given him the middle finger in the face as police were escorting the protester out of the stadium. The man was later arrested.

Over the previous eight months, Trump had held dozens of rallies attended by tens of thousands of people—several of them by as many as 30,000 people. Protesters had interrupted every one of Trump's rallies, yet not once had a Trump supporter physically attacked a protester before. Trump was not present in the stadium when the incident in North Carolina occurred, much less incite the incident. Nevertheless, the news media contrived to make it appear that Trump had incited the man to punch the protester, and had offered to pay the man's legal fees.

The news media did this by creating a split screen video that showed the 78-year old man punching the protester on the right side, and Trump speaking at a rally on the left side, saying to the crowd:

"Just knock the crap out of them, would you? I promise you, I will pay for the legal fees, I promise. I promise."

An observant viewer could have determined that two images were not of the same event because it is dark on the left side of the video that shows Trump speaking to a crowd, but daylight on the other side of the video showing the old man punching the protester. The statements Trump is shown saying to the crowd were made at a rally in Iowa more than a month before the incident in North Carolina. The statements were edited, taken out of context to distorted the tenor and meaning what Trump had said.

What Trump had said at the rally in Iowa, more than a month before the North Carolina incident, was clearly intended to be humorous, as even Katy Tur acknowledged at the time, saying that what Trump said sounded much worse on paper than at the rally, because it didn't capture the interaction between Trump and the crowd, the back and forth from which you could see he was kidding.

This is what Trump actually said at the Iowa Rally:

"This is the day we take our country back. So I've got a little notice, in case you see the security guys. The security guys said, Mr. Trump, there may be some people in the back with tomatoes in the audience. If you see somebody with a bag of tomatoes, just knock the crap out of them, would you? I promise you, I will pay for the legal fees, I promise. I promise."

It may not have been very presidential, but it was obviously crude, locker-room humor, a reference to the incident at an earlier rally in Iowa City, where a student actually threw a tomato at Trump:[87] Trump's comment was obviously not meant to be taken seriously. That's why the news media edited out the bit about the bag of tomatoes from Trump's statements, and consistently aired only Trump saying, "*Just knock the crap out of them*". For example, *CNN Politics* wrote under the caption, '*Trump Rallies Are Turning Violent*':

> "*At a rally in February, Trump told his supporters about protesters: 'Knock the crap out of them, would you? Seriously. OK? Just knock the hell -- I promise you, I will pay for the legal fees. I promise, I promise.'*"

CNN obviously had to edit out Trump's reference to bags of tomatoes otherwise it could not have used what Trump said to support its narrative about Trump inciting violence at his rallies.

Each network aired the edited, misleading video juxtaposing Trump's edited statements to the old man punching the protester throughout the next day, and continued to air it for days. Republican commentator S.E. Cupp, who never let an opportunity to demonize Trump pass, opined that "*Trump gives a nod and a wink to violence*", and added for good measure that Trump "*is not going to denounce the KKK*".

When interviewed about the North Carolina incident, Trump said he knew nothing about the matter, and had not agreed to pay the old man's legal fees. Still, CNN persisted in interpreting the original statement that Trump made a month earlier as having been

---

87 http://usuncut.com/politics/man-throws-tomato-at-donald-trump/

serious, and exaggerated it by referring to the North Carolina incident in its headline in the plural:

"Donald Trump wavers on paying legal fees of violent protesters."

It is, therefore, hardly surprising that when there was real violence at a Trump rally in Chicago on Friday, March 11, the weekend before Florida, the home state of Senator Rubio, and Ohio, the home state of sitting Governor Kasich, held winner-take-all primaries on March 15th, the news media blamed Trump for the violence instead of identifying who the perpetrators were and condemning them and the violence and mayhem they caused.

Trump was scheduled to speak at a rally held on the University of Illinois campus in Chicago. A crowd 6000 strong had gathered in the auditorium where Trump was scheduled to speak. Many had traveled across the Midwest, had taken time off work, and had waited up to 12 hours to hear Trump speak. There was a massive protest that threatened to turn violent, causing Trump to cancel the rally to defuse the situation.

Two videos showing policemen separating individuals poised for violent altercations inside the auditorium where Trump was scheduled to speak were aired throughout the evening by each cable news network in place of the networks' scheduled programs. CNN's video had "Live" written on the bottom right of the screen as it re-aired videos of incidents that had occurred hours earlier. The anchors airing the videos—Chris Mathews, Erin Burnette, Don Lemmon and others— commented on the same two videos throughout the evening, and interviewed Trump's opponents and law makers, asking them to comment on the rally. Everyone blamed Trump's rhetoric, not the protesters, for the violence. None of the anchors discussed who the protesters were or how the protest came about.

The cable news networks continued to make news out of the violence in Chicago throughout the weekend by airing and commenting on the same two videos they had aired on Friday night. The Monday morning talk shows also aired the same two videos without discussing who was responsible for the violence. It was not until Monday evening, the night before the all-important March 15 primaries that the provenance of the protest and violence was disclosed to the public by Bill O'Reilly[88] during his 8PM program, *The O'Reilly Factor*. The cable news networks never said a word about it on the air until the morning of the March 15 primaries when CNN's Chris Cuomo picked up on O'Reilly's story, and for the first time stated on *New Day*, the morning show he co-anchors, that the Chicago protest seemed to be professionally organized.

The Illinois University faculty and *Moveon.Org* had 50,000 people sign an on-line petition, and asked the college to cancel the Trump event. More than 9000 said on Facebook that they would protest at the rally if it wasn't cancelled: they included Bernie supporters and Black Lives Matter activists, who took part in the carefully organized plan to stop Trump from speaking.

The pretext for the request to cancel the Trump event was that at recent rallies Trump's supporters and security personnel had allegedly verbally and physically assaulted protesters. The letter to University officials read:

"We are deeply distressed that this event threatens to create a hostile and physically dangerous environment to the students, staff, faculty and alumni who come out to express their opposition."

---

88 http://www.billoreilly.com/video?chartID=556

The protesters at the rallies the letter referred to did more than express their opposition—their express intention was to prevent Trump from speaking— but the news media only showed them being ejected from Trump rallies, not the conduct they had engaged in before they were ejected. Nor did the news media ever invite legal experts to explain to the public what the right to protest actually entails, and, therefore, inform viewers that there is no right to enter private events, much less disrupt them or try to prevent people from speaking.

The University declined the petition, and in a statement from Chancellor Michael Amiridis explained,

> *"While the university is not endorsing Trump, it's renting out the venue to his campaign -- as it would any other political candidate that requested it."*

O'Reilly came to Trump's defense, saying:

> *"Throughout the week, far-left people ramped up a campaign to deny Donald Trump a forum, so it was no surprise on Friday that disruptive protesters entered the pavilion to shut Trump down and confront his supporters. Far-left agitators who do not believe in freedom of speech drove a situation that could have become violent, but the national media spun the story, demonizing Mr. Trump and his supporters, blaming the incident on 'inflammatory rhetoric' and 'racist thought'."*

O'Reilly aired video clips of interviews with protesters from which it was obvious that they had not come to the event to express opinions because when asked by reporters why or what they were protesting, the protesters couldn't answer.

A video was posted on Twitter in which a protester is seen confidently predicting that there would be violence inside the auditorium where Trump was scheduled to speak, and describing how the protesters had arranged to link arms to resist being taken down—which is exactly what a group of Black Lives Matter activist did at a recent Trump rally.

Katy Tur playing on the violence theme tweeted to her followers twice that the Sheriff's office in Lafayette, North Carolina had issued a statement that it was investigating whether Donald Trump had incited a riot and violated state law.

CHAPTER 21

Ides of March

• • •

THE FIRST PIECE NEWS ABOUT races held on March 15 was received at 7AM, just as people started going to the polls. It was learned that Trump had won the North Mariana Island caucuses by 73% of the vote, and captured all the island's nine delegates. But that was not the information Katy Tur tweeted to her followers.

Instead of reporting the result of the North Mariana caucus, Tur harked on the violence theme the Media had been milking all weekend, and tweeted that the Sheriff of Lafayette would not be seeking a "warrant" or "indictment" against Trump.

Her next tweet was a retweet of a CNN report captioned: "Trump wavers on paying legal fees for violent supporters." She followed that with another retweet of Michael Barbaro's tweet of a Politico article with the caption,

"Politico digs deep on Trump's campaign manager, finding unsavory incidents in his recent past".[89]

---

89 http://www.politico.com/story/2016/03/donald-trump-corey-lewandowski-220742 ...

In other words, Tur was tweeting to her followers a third hand 're-port' of facts she had not verified.

At about the time Tur was posting these tweets, a national poll showed Trump leading with 53% of the vote, the first time he had broken through the 50% mark. (Two other polls showed him in the lead with 43% & 44% of the vote, respectively.) Polling from Florida indicated that Trump had increased his lead by 6% despite the $15 million spent by SuperPacs on negative advertising against him in the week leading up to the March 15 Primaries. But Katy Tur never informed her followers of these facts about the candidate she was assigned to follow: she tweeted only information about violence.

As soon as the polls closed on Tuesday, the networks projected Trump the winner in Florida: he'd won 66 of Florida's 67 counties, and collected all 99 delegates in the winner-take-all state. Trump had defeated a popular former governor of the state, and its sitting Senator, but commentators lost no time trying to diminish Trump's achievement by calling Florida Trump's second home.

Rubio quickly gave a concession speech, and announced that his withdrawal from the race. Then came the much awaited projection that Kasich had won the Ohio primary. After that, all anyone on the air could talk about was a contested convention. Everyone was of one mind, and confidently predicted that Trump was highly unlikely to get the 1237 delegates needed for the nomination before the convention. Unrestrained speculation followed, tied to slanted reporting of election results, calculated to minimize how well Trump had done, with only an occasional, begrudging admission that, as Wolf Blitzer put it, *"it was a very good night for Trump"*.

John King, CNN's 'numbers man' went through several hypothetical scenarios about who might win the outstanding races, and concluded after every scenario that Trump needed to get 60% of the remaining delegates to get the 1237 needed to win the nomination, which, he opined, was possible but very unlikely. Jake Tapper, Rubio's communication director, and others repeated this incorrect statistic, and used it as the premise of their discussions about a contested convention. As if to underscore how absurd all this commentary was, Amanda Carpenter, a former communication director for Cruz, emphasized that that Cruz was the only other person besides Trump who could win, even though Cruz needed to get 74% of the remaining delegates to get to 1237, not 60%.

The delegate count published by independent sources on-line told a very different story.[90] There were 1079 delegates left after the March 15 Republican primaries. Trump had 661 delegates, and needed 576 delegates to win, which is 53%, not 60% of the remaining delegates. Cruz had 406 delegates, and needed 831 (77%) delegates to win. Kasich had 142 delegates, and couldn't get the1237 delegates required to win prior to the convention.

Cruz, after losing every race on March 15, declared that it was now a two-man race, and that he was the only one besides Trump who could win, as Kasich had been "mathematically eliminated" from the race. Cruz could not win as a practical matter: only Trump had a realistic chance of getting the 1237 delegates needed to win before the convention, but no one in the Media pointed that out. A contested convention, and the anti-Trump movement were the topics that dominated the discussion about the race—and the meeting scheduled for later in the week between hedge fund

90 https://www.google.com/?gws_rd=ssl#q=Republican+primaries&eob=m.09c7w0 /R/2/full/m.09c7w0/

managers and party apparatchik to see if they could agree on a plan to stop Trump.

Later in the day, President Obama announced that he was nominating Chief Judge Merrick Garland of the D.C. Circuit to replace Justice Scalia on the Supreme Court, which provided welcome relief to the stale cynicism and negativity with which all the news cable networks had flooded the airways the previous four days. Speculation about what Republican Senators might and might not do was interrupted by a call from Florida Governor Rick Scott to the Republican Party to respect the clear will of the voters, and unite behind Donald Trump. Would his endorsement open the floodgates to further endorsements? became, temporarily, the new topic of speculation.

But these were transient distractions, and the Media quickly returned to its speculations about a contested convention, in the course of which, it invented a new social reality: that Trump had "warned" or "threatened" that there would be riots if he had most of the delegates but fell short of 1237, and wasn't nominated at a contested convention. Here is how that false social fact was created.

Trump was interviewed by Chris Cuomo on CNN's *New Day* the day after the March 15 primaries, and Cuomo asked Trump about a contested convention. Trump opined that if he had 1100 delegates, and someone else had 500, and he was not nominated, he thought there could be a riot. The Media immediately seized on Trump's statement, and disingenuously linked it to the near riots in Chicago to continue its portrayal of Trump as responsible for the violence occurring at his rallies.

Trump's statement was repeated by CNN on each of its hourly news programs. Ashley Banfield, Wolf Blitzer, Brook Baldwin, Jake

Tapper all characterized Trump as "warning" about riots, never making it clear that he was merely offering an opinion in response to a question. Fox News's Shephard Smith went further, and said that Trump was "threatening" a riot.

The portrayal of Trump as warning or threatening riots if he was denied the nomination at a contested convention continued the following day. The bellicose Bob Barr from Georgia spoke of Trump threatening the kind of "violence" we'd recently seen at his rallies if there was a contested convention, and Trump wasn't nominated.

In fact, on the same day that Trump said he thought there could be riots if he was not nominated at a contested convention, Eli Stokolis and Alex Isenstadt of Politico made exactly the same prediction, and wrote:

> *"'Only in the minds of the delusional DC establishment is there a brokered convention at this point,' said Tony Fabrizio, a long-time GOP pollster who advised Rand Paul's campaign. And if the elites try and steal the nomination from Trump, the riots at the '68 Democratic Convention will look like a garden party.'"*[91]

The violence narrative was playing itself out as the campaigns inched towards the March 22 contests in Arizona and Utah, made its last gasp before the Arizona primary, after which the Media lost interest in the topic as it turned its attention to other contrived narratives with which to attack Trump.

---

91 http://www.politico.com/story/2016/03/trump-contested-convention-establishment-plans-220848#ixzz43620w38h

CHAPTER 22

More Violence

• • •

TRUMP HAD NO CHANCE IN Utah. Romney was making robocalls for Cruz, although wasn't endorsing him, and the governor of Utah endorsed Cruz the day before the caucuses. Trump held one rally at the Infinity Event Center in Salt Lake City on the Friday before the caucuses. Protesters tried to rush the door to the building but were blocked by police dressed in riot gear. Protesters pelted Trump supporters with rocks as they exited the building, and some of them tore down the security tent the U.S. Secret Service used to screen attendees before they entered the building. The media said nothing about who the violent protesters were, and did nothing to find out.

The next day there were protests in New York City while Trump held two rallies in Arizona. Crowds of demonstrators gathered outside Trump International Hotel on Central Park West just off Columbus Circle and marched the short distance down Fifth Avenue to Trump Tower. There was only a small skirmish when protesters started throwing water bottles at police, but it was quickly brought under control, and only three people were arrested. President Obama left on his historic trip to Cuba earlier that day, but an event that would ordinarily have dominated the news was overshadowed by races across the country, three thousand miles from the protests in New York.

Trump's first rally that day was in Fountain Hills, Arizona, and protesters blocked a road to the rally by chaining themselves to cars. Three people were arrested, and two cars towed away, after which the protesters quickly dispersed.

At the second rally in the Tucson Convention Center later in the day, Trump was repeatedly interrupted by protesters, some of whom engaged in physical altercations with Trump's supporters. There was also a standoff in the bleachers between about two dozen demonstrators and security officials, behind where Trump was standing. Trump turned to face the protesters as they were being escorted out, and told the crowd,

"These are not good people folks. They're not really protesters, they're agitators."

Still, no one in the Media held the protesters to account, or did anything to find out who they were.

Trump won the Arizona primary and collected all the State's 58 delegates. Cruz got all of Utah's 40 delegates as he won by more than 50% of the vote. The pace of the race then abruptly slowed. There were only two primaries in the next four weeks, two weeks apart: one in Wisconsin two weeks later (on April 5th), and one in New York two weeks after that (on April 19th). But the news was packed with other headlines after the Arizona and Utah primaries.

First, there were the terrorist attacks on Brussels in the early hours of the morning while the votes from Arizona & Utah were still being counted. Two bombs went off at the Brussels airport, closing air traffic for several days, and one at the Maelbeek subway station a block from the center of the European Union's headquarters. Thirty-one people excluding the terrorists were killed—four of them it was later learned were Americans— and more than two hundred injured.

Obama made brief remarks about the attack at a news conference in Cuba at which he called for the world to unite "against the scourge of terrorist", but failed to name the people responsible for the violence much to the consternation of many Republicans. Senator Ben Sasse of Nebraska denounced Obama's comments saying, *"Leadership is not found in platitudes that do not name our enemy"*.

Two days earlier, one of the terrorists involved in the attack on Paris on November 13, 2016 had been captured in Brussels, and was being interrogated by the Police when the attack occurred. As details of the attack, the identity and fate of the terrorists involved in the attack, and Europe's security problems were being discussed, Obama stole the headlines again, and again for the wrong reasons.

First, he attended a baseball game with Cuba's leader, Raoul Castro, where he could be seen smiling and waving to the crowd as the bodies in Brussels were still being counted. Then he flew to Argentina instead of the White House, as many believed he should have done, and justified his decision not to alter his schedule with the familiar argument that it would have played into the hands of the terrorists.

"The whole premise of terrorism is to try to disrupt people's ordinary lives. And one of my most powerful memories and one of my proudest moments as President was watching Boston respond after the marathon. ... That is the kind of resilience and the kind of

strength that we have to continually show in the face of these terror-ists" the President said.

He didn't convince his critics. Rudy Giuliani was expressing how they felt when he pointed out that to Belgians, a small country with a population less than New Jersey's, it was their 9/11.

"How would we have felt if after 9/11 we had seen the President of France smiling and waving to the crowd at a soccer match?" Giuliani asked.

But it got worse after the President got to Argentina. It was one thing not to alter his schedule, but quite another to be seen doing the Argentine Tango during a state dinner given in his honor, while bodies were still being picked off the streets of Brussels, and the wounded treated in its hospitals. The Media talked euphemistically about "optics", but it was more than an administrative snafu. It was an insensitivity that spoke volumes about the real character of our President.

Ted Cruz responded to the attack by saying he would place Muslim neighborhoods under surveillance, and came under fierce attack from New York City's Mayor de Blasio and Police Commissioner Bill Bratton. Cruz had lifted the idea from Trump, but got it wrong. After the Paris attack, Trump said that *'certain'* Mosques, not entire Muslim neighborhoods, should be placed on surveillance.

Although Trump had evinced knee jerk condemnation from the news media and its pundits, there was clear evidence that some mosques were preaching Jihad and radicalizing people. After the terrorist attacks on Paris, France's leading Iman, Hassan El Aloui announced that 100 to 160 mosques in France would be closed for preaching hatred and using takfiri speech.[92] The President of the German domestic intelligence agency, Hans-Georg Maassen, said that 90 mosques in German were under surveillance because of *"the threat to Germany posed by the 'Islamic State'"* through inciting jihad.[93]

---

92 http://www.aljazeera.com/news/2015/12/france-100-mosques-close-151202142023319.html

93 http://www.dw.com/en/german-intelligence-chief-around-90-mosques-under-surveillance/a-19229233

CHAPTER 23

From Violence to the Gutter

• • •

THE CAMPAIGN WAS THEN DRAGGED into the gutter by Liz Mair, founder of the Anti-Trump SuperPac, *Make America Awesome*, who had been fired by the Walker campaign the previous year for inappropriate comments she made about Iowa. She aired an advertisement in Utah about Trump's wife, Melania, with the caption, *"Meet Melania, Your Next First Lady"*.

The caption appeared below a picture of Melania, taken years earlier when she worked as a model, that appeared on the front cover of G.Q magazine and showed her lying naked on a couch with pillows covering her breasts and nether region. It was an artistic picture taken by a prominent photographer, but the gutter-snipe Mair tried to turn it into something salacious.

Trump was furious, and retorted with a tweet:

"Lyin' Ted Cruz just used a picture of Melania from a G.Q. shoot in his ad. Be careful, Lyin' Ted, or I will spill the beans on your wife!"

Trump's spokesperson, Katrina Pierson, later explained that by *"spilling the beans"* on Cruz's wife Trump was referring to all the policies Cruz's wife had supported at Goldman Sacks that Cruz was now claiming to be against. The news media greeted her explanation with incredulity.

Then Trump shot himself in the foot. Someone had sent him a tweet that had an unflattering picture of Ted Cruz's wife, Heidi, next to a beautiful picture of Melania Trump with the caption: *"A picture is worth a thousand words"*. Trump retweeted it, and created a firestorm. An indignant Ted Cruz called Trump a *"sniveling coward"* and his remark was aired by every news network throughout the news cycle for days. The Media wouldn't let it go, and continued to make news out of the retweet, and question Trump about it for more than a week.

Anderson Cooper asked Trump about the retweet at a town hall. Trump began his answer by pointing out that he didn't start the war about their wives, but Cooper cut him off.

"With respect," Cooper interjected, *"that's the answer of a five year old"*, and his putdown then became the news aired repeatedly by the networks for days.

The day after the races in Arizona and Utah, the National Enquirer ran a story alleging that Cruz had had extramarital affairs with five women, which created yet another uproar. Cruz vehemently denied the allegation, and accused Trump and his organization of being behind the story without a shred of evidence to support his accusation. The Media also implicated Trump in the story, also without a shred of evidence to support their position.

Jake Tapper jumped on the chance to make hay out of the story, but what neither he nor anyone else in the news media reported was that Rubio allies had been peddling the same story without success to various news organizations for at least six months.[94] Trump denied he had anything to do with the story, and said he hoped it was untrue, only to be mocked by the news media for saying something he could not possibly have meant.

Just when everyone thought it couldn't get worse for Trump, it did, and at the worst possible time: before the Wisconsin primary held on April 5th. Big news from the Justice Department could have buried the bad news for Trump, but the Media was determined not to let that happen.

---

94 http://www.thedailybeast.com/articles/2016/03/25/ted-cruz-affair-rumors-peddled-by-marco-rubio-s-allies.html

CHAPTER 24

Work It Baby

• • •

ON TUESDAY, MARCH 29, THE week before the Wisconsin primary, the Justice Department dropped its suit against Apple because the FBI had unlocked the iPhone of the San Bernardino shooter, Syed Rizwas Farook. It was big news that had the potential to change the war on terror.

The iPhone's security feature was threatening national security. It was providing an impenetrable shield the terrorist could to hide their communications about terrorist attacks behind, and impeding law enforcement's ability to gather intelligence about terrorist activities. Apple refused to help the justice department access the information on Farook's iPhone. It had the backing of all the nation's largest technology companies, and there seemed to be nothing anyone could do about it.

All that abruptly changed after Cellebrite, an Israeli forensic technology company located in New Jersey, successfully hacked into Farook's iPhone. It was a development with far reaching implications. The company's stock surged in anticipation that major police departments like the NYPD would be lining up outside Cellebrite's doors. How Apple's stock would be affected remained uncertain.

A story this important doesn't come along every day—but it was not the story with which Wolf Blitzer, CNN's $5 million a year chief anchor, began his 1PM news program, "*Wolf*" or his 5PM two-hour show, "*The Situation Room*". Like every other anchor of every news program on every other cable news network, Blitzer began both his programs with news that Trump's campaign manager, Corey Lewandowski, had been charged with one count of simple assault – others reported the charge as simple battery. The charge was based on the incident that had occurred on March 8, 2016 involving Michelle Fields.

Blitzer talked about the charge against Lewandowski for the first 37 minutes of his one-hour, 1PM program. He invited surrogates of every candidate – Cruz, Kasich, Clinton, Sanders – to comment on the charges. He specifically asked each candidate whether he or she would have fired Lewandowski, and they all said they would have. After Clinton's spokesperson, Brian Fallon, failed to give the answer Blitzer seemed to be hoping for, Blitzer put words into Fallon's mouth: was he saying that Trump bore responsibility for his campaign manager's actions? Blitzer asked.

Blitzer next asked a four-member panel to comment on Lewandowski's conduct. He specifically asked one of them, CNN's legal analyst, Jeffrey Tobin, for a legal opinion. Tobin began by listing the things one cannot do to another person, starting with "punch someone", even though Fields never alleged that Lewandowski had punched her.

Tobin said nothing about what reasonable actions a person in Lewandowski's position could lawfully take to protect Trump from possible threats. Nor did Tobin or Blitzer or any other member of the panel discuss whether there were any limits set on what reporters could legally do in their efforts to ask a candidate a question. The law defines "assault" as an intentional act by one person that creates an apprehension of an imminent harmful or offensive contact in another person, coupled with an apparent, present ability to cause the harm. Were they permitted to invade a candidate's personal space and make them feel threatened and unsafe?

The panel talked and talked and talked about everything except what Fields had actually alleged:

"Someone had grabbed me tightly by the arm and yanked me down. I almost fell to the ground, but was able to maintain my balance. Nonetheless, I was shaken."

The Fields incident took place at Trump's exclusive Florida club Mar-a-Lago. Trump released a surveillance video to the police that consisted of rapid sequence still frames that had captured the incident. One of the frames shows Field holding what looked like a pen in her left hand, and her left hand actually touching Trump's right hand. A subsequent frame shows Trump pulling his right arm away from Fields, and looking down at her hand. The next series of frames show Lewandowski pull Fields's left shoulder to the side so he could interject himself between Fields and Trump.

The video showed conclusively that what Fields alleged never happened: everyone agreed about that. Fields doesn't stumble or lurch, much less almost fall to the ground after Lewandowski touched her left shoulder as he brushed past her to interject himself between her and Trump, and she made no corrective body movement to maintain her balance. On the audio Tur released shortly after the incident,

Fields can be heard breathing normally, speaking in a normal tone of voice, making no excited utterances as she reacts verbally to the incident that had just occurred. The picture Fields tweeted showed a bruise on her left lower forearm, but the video of the incident shows Lewandowski touching Fields' left shoulder.

It was later revealed that the Secret Service had told Fields twice not to push through the security shield around Trump. A video released later showed a Secret Service agent directing Fields away from the group of people around Trump exiting the room, and Fields making her way through the group of people in defiance of the instructions.

Every hour thereafter, CNN began every newscast by re-airing the same story and the same commentary from Trump's political opponents, but omitted, as Blitzer had, to state what Fields had actually alleged—that she was forcibly almost yanked to the ground—and that was flatly refuted by the video the police released to the public.

The next day, CNN's Kate Bolduan began the eleven o'clock newscast by describing the incident as Lewandowski '*man handling*' a reporter. But she failed to report, as did Blitzer the next hour, and every other anchor on every other cable news network, that the *Washington Post* had reported that Mike Edmonson, a spokesperson for the prosecutor's office handling the case, had told the Post that prosecutors had not yet received the case file from the police, and had yet to determine how they would proceed. Nor did the cable news media report that Dave Aronberg, the prosecutor whose office was handling Fields's complaint, was a Democrat and former state senator, who was backing Hillary Clinton, and who donated $1,000 to her campaign in January and had been listed among Clinton's "Florida Leadership Council" since November, 2015.

After being accused of forcibly almost yanking Fields to the ground, Lewandowski said, "I never touched her, I have never even met her." It was obviously an expression made in response to being called a thug who had forcibly yanked Fields almost to the ground, but the Media interpreted Lewandowski's statement literally, and branded him a liar because he had made physical contact with Fields's left shoulder, as he moved to interject himself between her and Trump, and so had 'touched' her.

Trump was repeatedly questioned about the charges at interviews and town hall meetings, and criticized for standing by his campaign manager. Responses by Cruz saying that of course he would have fired Lewandowski were repeatedly aired and juxtaposed to Trump's statements that he would not fire Lewandowski because he had done nothing wrong. Trump said he knew it would be politically expedient to fire Lewandowski, but he simply couldn't do something that would destroy Lewandowski career. Trump described Lewandowski as a very good person with a beautiful family, and four wonderful children, and that he would stand by him because he was loyal to people who worked for him.

C: April Fool

• • •

CHAPTER 25

Then It Got Worse

• • •

JUST WHEN IT WAS LOOKING as if things could not possibly get worse, they did. Six days before the Wisconsin primary, Trump attended a town hall meeting hosted by MSNBC during which Chris Mathews managed to ensnare Trump in another fire storm, this time over abortion: specifically, whether a woman who has an abortion should be punished if abortion were made illegal—although Mathews never asked a straight question like that, nor did Trump give an answer like that.

The exchange began with a young woman in the audience asking Trump the following question about his position on women's issues:

"I have a question on women's rights, and what is your position on their right to choose and their reproductive health."

Trump: *"OK. Well, look, as you know I'm prolife, I think you know that…with three exceptions. Pretty much that's my stance. Is that OK. Do you understand…"*

The question was clearly selected to be a lead into a pre-planned attack on the unsuspecting Trump. Mathews took over before the woman could answer Trump, and began his interrogation with the following *non sequitur*:

Mathews: *"What should the law be on abortion?"*

Trump: *"Well, I have been prolife—"*

Mathews: *"I know. What should...I know the principle, and that's a good value, but what should be the law?"*

Mathews never asked Trump directly "should a woman who has an abortion be punished if abortion were made illegal"? He argued to the premise by *asserting* that if you are prolife you must want to ban abortion. He then got Trump to agree to the false logic of his next premise—if you want to ban abortion you must want to make it a crime or murder. Here is how Mathews got Trump to accept the false assumption that anyone who has a prolife position must believe that abortion is a crime, without ever actually asking Trump if he wanted to make abortion a crime:[95]

Mathews: *"I've never understood the prolife position. I've understood the principle. It's the taking of a human life as some people see it. But what crime is it?"*

Trump: *"Well, it's the taking of life—"*

Mathews cut Trump off, and didn't allow him to finish his thought. He went from *"what crime is it"* to *"should the woman be punished"*:

Mathews: *"Should the woman be punished...for having an abortion?"*

Trump: *"Ah, look—"*

---

95 https://www.youtube.com/watch?v=jGSttcyn2RI

Mathews cut Trump off again as he realized Trump wouldn't take the bait yet, so he switched from the woman being punished to '*abortion*' (sic) being punished.

> **Mathews**: "*This is not something you can dodge. If you say that abortion is a crime or abortion is murder you have to deal with it under the law. Should abortion (sic) be punished.*"

Trump wasn't trying to dodge anything, and he had also not said that an abortion was a crime or murder, but Mathews got Trump to agree that if abortion were illegal, there has to be some form of punishment for it.

> **Mathews**: "*…you're running for President of the United States, Chief Executive of the United States, do you believe in punishment for abortion as a principle? Yes or no, as a principle?*"

> **Trump**: "*The answer is that there has to be some form of punishment—*"

Mathews cut Trump off again before he could finish his answer. Having got him to say there had to be some form of punishment, Mathews dropped his voice and slipped in 'the woman':

> **Mathews**: "*For the woman?*"

> **Trump**: "*Yeah, there has to be some form—*"

Mathews cut Trump off again. Trump had only admitted to believing that there had to be some form of punishment if abortion were made illegal, but Mathews wanted to link 'punishment' to 'the woman', so cut Trump off to prevent him from expanding on his answer.

Mathews: "*Ten cents or ten years?*"

Trump: "*That I don't know.*"

Mathews: "*Why not?*

Trump: "*Because I don't know—*"

Mathews: "*Why not? You've taken positions on everything else.*

And I'm asking you what should a woman face—"

Trump: "*I am not going to do that—*"

Mathews: "*—if she chooses to have an abortion—*"

Trump: "*I am not going to do that—*"

Mathews: "*Why not?*"

Trump: "*Frankly, I do take positions on everything else, but it's a very complicated position—*"

Mathews: "*But you said you were broadly pro-life which means you want to ban it.*" (speaking over Trump)

Trump: "*But wait a minute, the Catholic Church is prolife—*"

Mathews: "*Don't talk about my religion—*"

It was obvious that Trump hadn't admitted to the opinion Mathews wanted to tag him with, so Mathews made one final all-out effort to bully the answer he wanted out of Trump:

Mathews: *"…You tell me what the law should be."*

Trump: *"You told me—"*

Mathews: *"Just tell me what the law should be—"*

Trump: *"I—"*

Mathews: *"You said you are prolife."*

Trump: *"I am prolife with exceptions—"*

Mathews: *"What does that mean?"*

Trump: *"I have not determined what the punishment should be."*

Mathews: *"Why not?"*

Trump: *"Because I haven't determined it."*

Mathews: *"When you decided to be prolife you should have thought about it."*

Mathews created the headlines for the next week as he knew he would. Every hour of every day each cable news network aired edited portions of the interview, and mischaracterized Trump's position saying, "Trump Says Women Who Have An Abortion Should Be Punished". The clarification Trump gave after the program was portrayed as Trump changing his position again. The exchange was a good illustration of the public forum the news media has created for exchanging ideas and the disingenuousness of its professed interest debating maters of public policy.

As if that wasn't enough, Trump then shot himself in the foot again by criticizing the economic policies of Wisconsin's popular governor, Scott Walker, who had won a recall election in his state, and who had endorsed Cruz. Trump called the talk show host, Charlie Sykes, the best known and most influential of the conservative radio talk show hosts in Wisconsin, who had been attacking Trump mercilessly on the air for months, and was a 'Never Trump' person. Apparently no one in the Trump campaign had warned Trump, and Sykes himself was so surprised that Trump would agree to an interview that his first question to Trump was:

"Mr. Trump, before you called into my show, did you know that I'm a #NeverTrump guy? And I give you credit either way for it."

"No, I didn't know that, but I also assume you're an intelligent guy, I know you're an intelligent guy, and you understand what's going on," Trump replied.

Sykes grilled Trump for ten minutes about his retweet of the unflattering picture of Cruz's wife, and his criticism of Walker's economic plan. The grilling was generally considered to have damaged Trump. So it came as no surprise to anyone that two polls showed Cruz in the lead by ten percent— 40% to 30% and 42% to 32%— or that Cruz then over-performed, and won the state's primary by 48% of the vote on April 5th.

The news media was delirious: Wisconsin was where Trump had finally been stopped. There was no way that Trump could now win the nomination outright, and there would be a fight at the Convention in Cleveland that Cruz was poised to win once the delegates were 'released' after the first ballot, and could vote for anyone.

The Wisconsin primary came after the worst two weeks for Trump imaginable. It started with the Florida police charging Trump's campaign manager with assaulting a reporter. Then Cruz and the news media accused Trump of being responsible for the salacious National Enquirer article about Cruz, which was taken as proof of his coarseness and vulgarity. Then Trump shot himself in the foot not once, but twice: first by re-tweeting an unflattering picture of Cruz's wife, then by criticizing Scott Walker's economic policies. Then came his disastrous answer to Matthews's hypothetical 'gotcha' questions about abortion at a town hall meeting, and just for good measure, Trump shot himself in the foot a third time by calling into, and agreeing to be interviewed by a Never Trumper— Wisconsin's influential conservative talk show host, Eric Sykes.

Astonishingly, given all that, Trump got 35% of the vote, won two districts, and picked up 6 of the 42 delegates. Kasich, who had been projected to do well in the State, got only 14% of the vote. But few in the Media commented on the collapse of the Kasich vote or Trump's surprisingly strong showing. The headline the next day was that Cruz had trounced Trump in Wisconsin, and the Media dubbed April 5th *"Turnaround Tuesday"*.

Wisconsin had proved to be Cruz's firewall, and had reset the race. Wisconsin had exposed Trump's weaknesses, and Trump had been stopped. Time magazine featured Cruz on its front page with the caption, *"Likeable Enough"*. The Media's near delirium was palpable, and it did little to try to conceal it.

CHAPTER 26

Home Sweet Home

• • •

NEW YORK, TRUMP'S HOME STATE, was the next primary. All the polls were showing Trump leading by 25%-30%, and everyone knew Trump would win his home state, but the real question was how many delegates would he get?

New York had 27 districts, and 95 total delegates: each district had three delegates, and there were 14 at large delegates. Winning the state by more than 50% of the vote would only get Trump the states 14 at large delegates. He would have to win each of the 27 districts by more than 50% to get each district's three delegates.

The new media kept telling everyone that Cruz tended to overperform his poll numbers, and Trump to underperform them, and the state was favorable to the state's moderate republicans. So Kasich and Cruz could chip away at Trump, district by district, and erode his support, just as his support had eroded in Wisconsin. It was given credence by the state's former governor, George Pataki, who agreed that Trump would probably win the state but added,

"I think Ted Cruz has a real shot of surprising and doing really well."

CNN's John King, Fox News's Bill Hammer, and MSNBC's Steve Kornacki—the three news networks' 'numbers men'— went through every conceivable permutation to show that Trump could win the New York state, but still fall short of the of number of delegates Trump needed to win in New York to retain any chance of getting the 1237 delegates he needed to win the nomination outright on the first ballot.

The front page of the New York Daily New quickly put an end to the speculation about how well Cruz might do in New York. Cruz had scheduled a rally in the Bronx: no one showed up to Cruz's rally, and those that did booed him. The next day's headlines in the Daily News told Cruz how he could get out of the Bronx:

Take the FU Train, Ted

It hadn't forgotten Cruz's comments about 'New York values'.

Then came Colorado. Back in August, 2015, two months after Trump entered the race, and with the approval of the RNC, Colorado decided that it would not have a vote at all—i.e. not hold caucuses or a primary: state party officials, not the voters, would choose the delegates at a state convention. Cruz picked up all the state's 34 delegates, and shortly afterwards, the state party tweeted, *"We did it. #NeverTrump"*.

Trump was outraged, and called the system "rigged" and crooked. Paul Manafort, his newly appointed campaign manager, described Cruz's campaign as using *'Gestapo tactics'* to get delegates. Some in the news media, like *Morning Joe's* Joe Scarborough, agreed, but most ridiculed Trump's claims about the system being rigged.

Trump knew the rules and they haven't changed, they said, and Trump had been simply out-maneuvered by Cruz's superior organization: Cruz was *"cleaning Trump's clock"* is how Steve Kornacki gleefully put it. Trump was complaining because he'd lost: if he had won, he wouldn't be complaining about the system. It was a simple as that.

Trump's critique of the delegate selection process became the narrative for the following week until it was temporarily interrupted by the untimely death of Prince on Thursday, April 21, 2016 from what was later determined to be a drug overdose. There was now near unanimous agreement in the news media that Trump couldn't get the 1237 delegates he needed to win the nomination on the first ballot—and viewers were told that 'fact' several times every day.

MSNBC's legal analyst, Ari Melber, then came up with a new argument with which to discredit Trump's complaints about the delegate selection process. Trump had actually *benefitted* from the delegate system he was railing against because it had given him a "22% bonus", Melber argued.

Trump had won 37% of the primary votes cast, but had picked up 45% of the delegates awarded, which meant that for each percentage point of total primary votes Trump won, he picked up 1.22 percent of the delegates (45%÷37%), whereas Cruz had only received 1.14 percent of the delegates for each percentage point of the primary votes he had won.

Brilliant! Katy Tur and the other MSNBC reporters on the campaign trail, said, and gleefully tweeted references to Melber's article. It instantly became the argument of the moment, and repeated unthinkingly by pundits like S.E. Cupp and others in the Media, as well as politicians and Trump's opponents many times a day, but it was a mendacious argument.

The fact that Trump had a higher proportion of the delegates awarded than of the votes cast didn't mean the process benefitted *him*. It simply reflected the fact that the Republican Party decided not to use a proportional method of allocating delegates in many states, and Trump had won many more states than Cruz. Cruz also had a higher proportion of delegates than votes (a 14% "bonus"), but not quite as high as Trump because he had won far fewer states than Trump. It was a simple as that.

By definition, the percent of the delegates awarded to a candidate will only equal the percent of the votes won by that candidate if the state awards delegates proportionately. But in many states, the Republican Party does not award delegates proportionately, and the winner of such a state, whoever it is, will, by design, get a higher proportion of delegates than votes. That's why Senator Cruz got 85% of the delegates in Wisconsin (36/42), despite winning only 48% of the vote.

Nor was the method of allocating delegates the basis of Trump's complaint about the system being rigged. He called the system corrupt because the voters in Colorado were not given an opportunity to vote at all, not because a disproportionate number of delegates were awarded to Cruz. Trump didn't complain about Wisconsin, where Cruz won 48% of the vote and 85% of the delegates. Trump was complaining about party bosses deciding who got delegates in the state, who was qualified to be a delegate, and who would be selected to be a delegate in districts that Trump had won.

Cruz's tactic was to try to stop Trump getting the 1237 delegates needed to win on the first ballot at the Republican Convention in

Cleveland, and then rig the system so he would be favored on a second or third ballot. He was rigging the system by having delegates in districts that Trump won replaced by individuals who supported Cruz, so that after the first ballot, when delegates were free to vote for any candidate, they would vote for Cruz. This is what Paul Manafort was referring to as 'Gestapo tactics'.

The narrative abruptly changed during the second week leading up to the New York primary. Trump was giving a speech to a crowd of 20,000 people in a convention center in Pittsburgh on April 13, 2016, six days before the New York Primary. Fox News was airing the rally but abruptly interrupted it at about 7:30 PM with Breaking News:

Politico has reported that Lewandowski would not be prosecuted.

The news media had egg on its face. Two weeks earlier, the news media had saturated the airways with news that Lewandowski had been charged, and before Lewandowski had even been indicted on the charge against him, the news media had effectively convicted Lewandowski in the court of public opinion by repeatedly airing comments of Trump's opponents denouncing Lewandowski.

The Media's highly paid anchors—Wolf Blitzer, Anderson Cooper, Jake Tapper, Chris Mathews, Rachel Maddow, and more—had misled the public by failing to inform it that Lewandowski had not actually been indicted, only charged by the police. At the time they were asking Trump's opponents if they would have fired Lewandowski, prosecutors hadn't even received Lewandowski's case file from the police. It was another bedrock example of how the news media misleads the public and creates false impressions in the public's mind with statements that are factually accurate but incomplete.

The truth rarely catches up with the lie. The day after Politico reported that Trump's campaign manager would not be prosecuted, not a single cable news network began a single program with the news that Corey Lewandowski would not be prosecuted, notwithstanding that two weeks earlier each one had started their each newscast every day with news that Trump's campaign manager had been charged with one count of battery by the police. In its ruthless pursuit of making news and getting ratings, the news media gave no thought to what it might be doing to Lewandowski's wife and four children back home in New Hampshire.

As soon as the polls closed on Tuesday evening, April 19, 2016, each network projected Trump the winner. But how many delegates would he get? It didn't take long to know the answer. Trump was going to win by a landslide, and get at least 89 of the state's 95 delegates. Cruz didn't pick up a single delegate, and, like Kasich, he was now mathematically eliminated from the race—i.e. unable to get 1237 delegates needed even if he picked up every one of the remaining delegates.

Unbowed by his bad loss, Cruz told his supporters,

"I'm not going to get 1237 delegates before the Convention, but nor will Donald. The big news of the day is that Trump won his home state," Cruz said sarcastically.

His surrogates lost no time 'spinning' the loss by saying, *"Cruz won more votes in Wisconsin than Trump did in New York"* to try to discount the enormity of Trump's win and Cruz's loss. It was true that Cruz got about 5,000 more votes in Wisconsin than Trump got in New York, but Wisconsin was an open primary in which independents could vote, and New York was a closed primary, in which only Republicans could vote, and New York was a blue state that did not have many Republicans. It was an example of how the meaning conveyed by a true fact can be false.

CHAPTER 27

The Northeast Primaries

• • •

ATTITUDES CHANGED PERCEPTIBLY AS THE news media shifted its attention to Trump's lead in the five states slated to vote on April 26, 2016, the week after the New York primary: Connecticut, Delaware, Maryland, Pennsylvania, and Rhode Island. Trump was leading in each state by double digits—by more than twenty points in most of them—and Cruz was running third in many of them. What was thought highly unlikely if not impossible only a week earlier, now seemed more and more probable: Trump could very well get the 1237 delegates he needed to win the nomination on the first ballot. An internal memo from the Trump camp said he might get 1400 delegates.

Late on the Sunday, before Connecticut, Delaware, Maryland, Pennsylvania, and Rhode Island held their primaries, Cruz and Kasich announced that they had forged an alliance to increase the chances of stopping Trump getting the 1237 delegates he needed to clinch the nomination on the first ballot: they would both focus their campaign efforts solely on the states they were most likely to win. Kasich closed his two offices in Indiana, canceled scheduled campaign appearances, and would tell his supporters in Indiana to vote for Cruz, in exchange for Cruz not campaigning in Oregon and New Mexico, and telling his supporters to vote for Kasich. By the next day the alliance was already crumbling as Kasich declined to tell his supporters not to vote for him in Indiana. Perhaps it was a hint of why, despite his blue ribbon resume, Kasich could not get any traction with voters and so few establishment Republicans endorsed him.

On the day of the New England primaries, *Morning Joe* aired interviews with a number of Trump supporters who attended the massive rally the night before in Wilkes-Barre, Pennsylvania. They weren't uneducated, uninformed, angry, resentful working class white men—the news media's caricature of the typical Trump supporter throughout the primaries. They were upbeat, and exuded energy and enthusiasm. Many were middle and upper middle class, and well spoken. They spoke as if with one voice when asked why they were voting for Trump. *'He's authentic.' 'He's not a politician, he's not a lawyer.' 'He tells it like it is.' 'He's aggressive. That's America.'* Joe Scarborough described the impression created by these spontaneous interviews as: *"it looked like a $100 million Ad buy"*.

Scarborough praised Trump's ability to read an audience, but missed the larger point. Trump did more than read his audience: he understood before others the mood of an electorate devastated by loss of jobs, falling living standards, unaffordable colleges, and loss of houses by many during the financial crisis. Aptly described by his son, Donald Jr., as a *'blue collar billionaire'*, Trump understood the soul of America, and America saw him as embodying the quintessentially American 'can do', 'kick ass', 'show-me-your-stuff", 'never back down from a challenge' confident swagger they yearned to recapture. He was upbeat about American: it was infectious, and it made them upbeat about him.

Punditry was in full swing as the Northeastern states— Connecticut, Delaware, Maryland, Pennsylvania and Rhode

Island—went to the polls. All the talk was about Indiana, the new fire wall. Cruz and the Anti-Trump movement were pouring resources into the state hoping to stop Trump there. Partisans like Cruz's fired communication director, Rick Perry, and National Review editor, Rick Lowry, were comparing Indiana to Wisconsin, and talking up Cruz's chances in Indiana based on Cruz's late surge and big win in Wisconsin— but they were ignoring a crucial difference. Scott Walker, the popular governor of Wisconsin, had endorsed Cruz, and the entire Republican Establishment, including influential conservative radio talk show hosts were all backing Cruz. That was not the case in Indiana, whose governor said he wouldn't be endorsing anyone before the primary.

Bill Kristol, Editor of The Weekly Standard, who has an astonishing record of wrong prediction, was still pushing the possibility of an independent run by an establishment candidate. He admitted that it would be difficult, but not impossible for someone to get on the ballot in most states at this late stage, only there was too much resignation and fatalism for that to happen, he lamented. The country deserved better than Trump and Clinton, and the slow moving car crash that we were watching, he opined.

"Cruz might try a hail Mary," he suggested, and name Carly Fiorina as his running mate. Cruz could then show up with her in Indiana on Thursday, and present a ticket to the voters. But if Trump is to be stopped, he admitted that Indiana would have to deliver a strong delegate majority to Cruz.

Trump was leading in each of the Northeast states by double digits, and was expected to win all five states. But the size of his victories exceeded even the wildest expectations. He won each of the five states by more than 50% of the vote, and two of them by more than 60%. Trump outperformed his poll numbers by 10%, and took 111 of the 118 pledged delegates. Steve Kornacki called them "monster wins".

Trump won each of the 67 counties in Pennsylvania, which made it all but certain that he would win all the 54 unbound delegates in that state. Cruz didn't win a single county. Still, the *New York Times* couldn't help itself, and described the result with the headline:

"Trump Narrows Chances for Cruz and Kasich"

The *Washington Post*'s headline was more apposite:

"Trump's Sweep is Another Humiliating Defeat for Media and Political Elites"

And for the first time, *The Washington Post* showed real insight when it described the state of the race:

> *"Trump's story is about more than a first-time candidate's stunning rise. It is also about the humiliating defeat suffered by an increasingly isolated political and media class who still do not understand the causes and scope of Trump's populist revolt."*

But the Post's analysis of Trump's success was wide of the mark. *"Washington insiders and media moguls"* did more than *"misread the mood of working-class voters and their attraction to the populist message championed by Trump"*: they failed completely to understand the basis of Trump's appeal. Trump also didn't *"cruise[] to lopsided victories in Pennsylvania, Connecticut, Rhode Island, Delaware and Maryland"* simply because his message on trade, taxes and immigration that *"undermine[d] Republican orthodoxy resonated with GOP primary voters so strongly"*. He cruised to victory because Trump was restoring the image many Americans have of themselves and their country.

Trump did more than attract working class voters: he won every demographic group. He won with very conservatives, moderates, evangelicals, suburban women, college educated, high school educated, and he won every age group. The notion that most of Trump's voters were non-college educated, angry working-class white men was a news media created myth. Most of Trump's supporters were not college graduates simply because most of the general population are not college graduates.

Despite his landslide win in New York, and then landslide wins in five Northeastern states, the Media continued its unrelenting negative reportage about Trump, and speculations about how he could be stopped at the Republican Convention in Cleveland.

CHAPTER 28

Indiana: Cruz's Last Stand

• • •

CRUZ SPENT THE DAY OF the Northeast primaries in Indiana, a state *"in which basketball is church and Bobby Knight is the pastor"*, as Steve Kornacki put it. So, not surprisingly, Cruz staged a Media event in the evening in the very basketball court in which the film *Hoosiers*, starring Gene Hackman, was filmed, and re-enacted a scene from that film, as the results were showing Trump inching towards landslide wins in all five Northeastern states. But Cruz muffed the show he put on by referring to a basketball hoop as a basketball ring.

Hoosiers is about a failed basketball coach who is hired as a high school coach in a small Indiana town, and coaches the team to the championship. In the film, Hackman has his players measure the height of basketball hoop.

"How far?" Hackman asks his players.
"Ten feet," they reply.
"Ten feet. I think you'll find it's the same height as our gym back in Hickory."

Trump had announced that the day after the Northeast primaries he would be giving a major foreign policy speech in Washington.

In order to deflect attention from that speech, and Trump's landslide wins, Cruz told the Media the morning after the Northeast primaries that at 4PM that day, he would be making a major announcement. And in the afternoon, as predicted, Cruz announced that he had picked Carly Fiorina as his running mate—a bizarre move coming on the heels of losses in five primaries that eliminate Cruz mathematically from the race.

Cruz made his announcement with a rambling speech full of hyperbole, and Fiorina followed with an 'acceptance' speech that was also too long and replete with clichés and sentimentality. Cruz had told the crowd that his young children 'adored Carly', and Fiorina sang the song she told the crowd she sang to Cruz's children on Cruz's bus. As stagecraft, the event fell flat. The length of the speeches seemed to have sapped any genuine energy there may have been in the room, as the crowd's cheering sounded tepid and manufactured.

The contrast with the energy of the Trump rally that followed it could not have been greater. The legendary Hosiers coach, Bobby Knight—who is a "God" in Indiana, and known affectionately as "the general"— endorsed Trump, and fired up the crowd with a locker-room speech in which he described Trump as

> *"the most prepared man in history to step in as president of the United States"* and telling the crowd *"You will be helping our government take the first step toward what all of us want our government to be like."*

Trump responded with heartfelt appreciation, saying,

> *"That's a great man. That guy knows how to win. I love the attitude."*

Later that evening, the two appeared at a Town Hall hosted by Fox News with Greta van Susteren, host of *On the Record*. Many agreed that it was one of those rare endorsements that could make a difference.

Earlier in the day, Trump had given a foreign policy speech in Washington at the Center for National Interest. The speech received high praise not only from Trump supporters like Ann Coulter, who, with characteristic hyperbole, called it the *"greatest foreign policy speech since Washington's farewell address"*, and Laura Ingraham, who called it *"one of the most consequential foreign policy speeches since 1981"*, but also from neutral observers like four-star General Barry McCaffrey, who had been critical of Trump's comments in the past, saying that *"this time he hit it out of the park"*. Grover Nordquist called the speech *"sober, thought-through"*; former Virginia governor Jim Gilmore, called it *"very good"* and as *"responding to the concerns of the American people"*; and, perhaps most significantly, the Chairman of the Senate Foreign Relations Committee, Bob Corker of Tennessee, said he was *"very pleased"*, and described the speech as *"full of substance...very, very good"*.

Former House Speaker Newt Gingrich called Trump's speech a *"serious foreign policy speech...worth reading and thinking about"*, but correctly predicted, *"it will be ridiculed by Washington elites because it challenges their assumptions"*. And it was—as "incoherent" and "contradictory", but no one pointed out the incoherence or contradictions in the speech. The following morning, MSNBC described the reaction to Trump's speech as "mixed", but CNN's *New Day*, predictably led the charge against the speech with the headline:

"Trump's America First Foreign Policy Draws Criticism Across the Political Spectrum".

To promote CNN's viewpoint, Chris Cuomo picked an unsuccessful former Democrat Presidential candidate and Hillary Clinton supporter, General Wesley Clark, Supreme Allied Commander, Europe, of NATO from 1997 to 2000, to disparage Trump's foreign policy proposals. But Clark made such heavy weather of it that his criticisms may well have backfired, and reflected well on the speech in the eyes of undecided voters.

Clark said he was glad that Trump wasn't going to start any wars, and that, if he had to, he would have clear objectives. Clark also approved of Trump's rejection of 'nation building' saying *'we're not very good at that'*. But then Clark dismissed Trump's determination to make our allies pay the fair share of the cost of their own defense, saying that every President going back to Dwight Eisenhower had tried to do just that.

Clark unwittingly played into Trump's strong suit, and squarely framed the questions about his foreign policy proposals as one of competence: could Trump succeed where other Presidents had failed. Clark's answer was weak and incoherent:

"One of the things that bothers me the most in Mr. Trump's speech is this idea that he, personally, could redirect America's foreign policy. You know, this isn't a real-estate negotiation. It's not something you can sit down across the table. You're dealing with long-term national interests, and a set of allies that we have worked with for sixty years. They expect consistency, they expect stability, and this country has long-term interests. So trying go in and do it like a hotel deal in Moscow…I'll put it here, and you'll give me this…might work on the margins of some small agreement, but as the basis of stable, long-term relationships, and heading off the conflicts we're

heading toward with China and Russia, uh, uh. We've got big chal-
lenges with China and Russia, and you can't duck those challenges
by calling on your allies to spend more on defense."

Clark was assuming that by asking our allies to spend more, America
would somehow be "ducking" the challenges *"we're heading toward*
with China and Russia". He also assumed that the techniques of effective negotiations are subject dependent, and they are not. But
most dangerously, Clark assumed that long-term relationships are
fixed in stone, and cannot through negotiations grow and develop.
This seems to be the kind of thinking Trump was referring to in his
speech when he said he intended to:

"look for talented experts with approaches and practical ideas, rath-
er than surrounding myself with those who have perfect résumés
but very little to brag about except responsibility for a long history
of failed policies and continued losses at war. We have to look to new
people. We have to look to new people because many of the old people
frankly don't know what they're doing, even though they may look
awfully good writing in The New York Times or being watched on
television."

The next day Trump held a rally in Costa Mesa, South of Los Angeles
that turned violent. Protesters outside the amphitheater where
Trump was addressing a crowd several thousand strong smashed a
police car, threw stones and beer bottles, and about twenty of them
were arrested. A Trump supporter had a bloodied face, but there were
no serious injuries. Police on horses eventually cleared the crowds.

All afternoon the next day, the networks televised protesters
as they gathered outside the Hyatt Regency Hotel in Burlingame

California, where Trump was scheduled to speak to the California GOP Convention, rushed towards the hotel's door, tussled and shoved police who were blocking them from entering the building, and pushing them back with their batons. The protesters tore down barriers in their attempt to reach the hotel's entrance, and blocked off the road in front of the hotel in their attempt to stop Trump from speaking. Some protesters made it into the building, and could be seen through the glass door tussling with personnel in the hotel's lobby.

The cameras showed Trump's motorcade stop by a concrete median in the road behind the hotel, his entourage get out of their cars, walk along the median, cross the road, and enter the hotel through the back entrance. Trump's speech was delayed. The news media attributed the delay to the protest, speculating that organizers were waiting for the police to clear the building of the protesters that had managed to get inside, and even that Trump's speech might be canceled, as it had been the previous month in Chicago.

As they waited for Trump to speak, the television anchors filled the time by reading out loud some of the more incendiary signs the protesters were carrying, and comparing the protest with the more violent one on the previous night. The anchors characterized the protest as an exercise of the democratic right to free speech and to protest, but never informed viewers of what kind of protest the First Amendment to the U.S. Constitution allowed. The anchors again made no attempt to determine who the protesters were, and not once did the television anchors or reporters condemn the violence.

The commentary was very critical of Trump, not the protesters. Without actually saying so, the commentators described Trump as a divisive figure who had engendered antipathy with his comments about illegal immigrants and his immigration policies, and implied that Trump and his supporters were somehow responsible for the violence.

As they showed protesters gathering, the networks focused their narrative on Trump's unfavorability rate among women, African-Americans and Hispanics, and invited comments from several pundits and partisans on Trump's chances of winning a general election against Hillary Clinton. Never the less, several Trump supporters at the rally were Mexican-Americans opposed to illegal immigration, but only Fox News interviewed them.

Going into the weekend, there were mixed messages about the race. Governor Pence changed his mind, and announced that he was endorsing Cruz on a radio talk show hosted by the person who had prosecuted Mike Tyson for rape in Indiana twenty years earlier. Tyson had endorsed Trump, who touted the endorsement, which only gave the news media more ammunition with which to attack Trump as sexist.

But Pence sent somewhat of a mixed message by praising Trump effusively before he actually endorsed Cruz. Katy Tur called the endorsement a '*blow*' to the Trump campaign, but since she didn't actually ask anyone involved in the campaign about the endorsement, she didn't actually know the campaign's view, and was expressing a conjecture, although representing it as a 'fact'.

Indiana voters received more conflicting messages the day before the Pence endorsement. The State's leading newspaper, The Indiana Star, didn't endorse anyone, but said that Kasich, would be the best choice: former House Speaker, John Baynor, called Cruz 'Lucifer in the flesh'. To add to the uncertain mood, the predictions of Larry Sabato, a professor of political science at the University of Virginia, predicted a landslide victory for Hillary Clinton against Trump.

CHAPTER 29

The Last Hurrah

• • •

THE TALK SHOWS ON THE Sunday before the Indiana primary continued the Media's relentlessly negative coverage of Trump by interviewing Trump's detractors and opponents, like failed Presidential candidate, Lindsey Graham; failed New Jersey Republican Gubernatorial candidate, Steve Lonegan, who was backing Cruz; former Defense Secretary, Bob Gates; National Review journalist, John Fund; The National Journal's Ron Fournier, New York Times's Thomas Friedman, Presidential historian, Doris Goodwin, and others. They were asked to comment on Trump's foreign policy speech and unfavorability rates.

Bob Gates kicked off his attack on Trump with the false statement that Trump was asking our allies *"to pay for everything"*: Trump was actually only asking them to pay their fair share. Gates said his main concern was that Trump didn't understand the difference between a business deal and dealing with sovereign nations, and that he didn't listen, and thought he knew everything. Gates's opinion was flatly contradicted by what Javier Palomarez, the CEO of the Hispanic Chamber of Commerce, had said about Trump when they met back in September, 2015: that Trump was very respectful, and listened much more than he spoke at their meeting.

During his interview with John Dickerson, Lindsey Graham repeated the vitriolic diatribe he had used against Trump while Graham was still in the race, predicting that Trump would bring ruin on the Republican Party, and cause it to lose the Senate and House.

On MSNBC's *Meet The Press*, Chuck Todd took several statements from Trump's foreign policy speech, and declared them contradictory without explaining the supposed contradictions. The discussion between Fournier, Friedman, Goodwin and MSNBC White House correspondent Kristin Welker that followed bordered on the incoherent. One thing was clear: they were all horrified by the thought of a Trump Presidency, and agreed with Friedman that a Trump Presidency was only one terrorist attack in October away.

Hard as it is to believe, but the thing Ron Fournier found most 'scary' about Trump was that he had called ISIS a "phenomenon". Doris Kearns wondered how the public could be asked to approve military intervention should that be necessary if the President was being "unpredictable". Friedman called Trump's foreign policy speech "unnerving", and everything his critics said it was, but promptly acknowledged that it was difficult to have a coherent foreign policy today because the public wanted America to solve problems but also to stay out of the way. The rest of the group nodded vigorously in agreement.

Monday was Cruz's last hurrah. He scheduled ten appearances around the state, and Governor Pence campaigned with him: Carly Fiorina held separate campaigns around the state. Michael Reagan, President Reagan's eldest son, urged everyone to vote for Cruz.

But Trump was not to be outdone. Digger Phelps, Notre Dame's former basketball coach, endorsed Trump at a huge rally in South Bend. Earlier that day Notre Dame's former football coach Lou Holtz gave his endorsement to Trump.

The polls opened at 6AM on Tuesday, May 3rd, but Cruz wasn't done with campaigning. With the polls showing Trump well ahead, and a loss in Indiana looming large, Cruz unleashed a diatribe against Trump that was so vitriolic and extreme that it had many wondering if Cruz had reached some kind of a personal breaking point.

He began with the accusation that Trump had accused his father of being involved in the assassination of President Kennedy, which was untrue. He used it as justification for doing something he hadn't done for the entire campaign:

"I'm going to tell you what I really think of Donald Trump," he told reporters. *"This man is a pathological liar. He doesn't know the difference between truth and lies. He lies practically every word that comes out of his mouth. And in a pattern that I think is straight out of a psychology textbook, his response is to accuse everybody else of lying."*

"Donald will betray his supporters on every issue. If you care about immigration, Donald is laughing at you. And he's telling the money-eyed elites he doesn't believe what he's saying. He's not going to build a wall," Cruz told reporters.

He called Trump a *"bully"*, *"amoral"*, *"a serial philanderer"*, and *"a narcissist of a level the country has never seen before"*. He argued that Trump has a problem with women because he is insecure.

"I want everyone to think about your teenage kids. The president of the United States talks about how great it is to commit adultery, how proud he is, describes his battle with venereal disease as his own Vietnam — that's a quote, by the way, on the Howard Stern Show. Do you want to spend the next five years with your kids bragging about infidelity?" Cruz asked, rhetorically.

He ended by an appeal to Indiana voters, telling them only they could save the country from Trump.

"I would say to the Hoosier state, the entire country is depending on you. The entire country is looking to you right now. It is only Indiana that can pull us back. It is only the good sense and good judgment of Indiana that can pull us back. We are staring at the abyss. If Indiana does not act, this country could well plunge into the abyss. I don't believe that's who we are. We are not a proud, boastful, self-centered, mean-spirited, hateful, bullying nation."

The networks aired Cruz's diatribe in its entirety every hour throughout the day, and invited Cruz supporters and Trump's critics to comment on Cruz's statements on the air. But MSNBC and CNN went further: they repeated Cruz's false allegation that Trump had accused his father of being involved in Kennedy's assassination, and made it the narrative of the day. MSNBC and CNN repeated the allegation every hour until it was eventually taken up by Fox News as well, after Shephard Smith concluded his 3PM newscast. It was another news media overreach.

What Trump actually did was to reply to an attack on him by Cruz's father (which neither MSNBC nor CNN mentioned) and in the course of his reply referred to an article in which Cruz's father was ostensibly pictured with Lee Harvey Oswald, and Trump asked "why isn't anyone looking into that?"

The article appeared in The National Enquirer on April 20, 2016. It showed a picture of Lee Harvey Oswald standing in front of, and to the left of a man in a white shirt, who was handing out leaflets for the *Fair Play for Cuba Committee* outside the International Trade Mart in New Orleans on August 16, 1963. The man in the white shirt was never identified by the Warren Commission that investigated Kennedy's assassination, but the Enquirer claimed it had determined through photo analysis that the man was in fact Rafael B. Cruz, Cruz's father. The Media didn't investigate the claim, and the story was ignored until Trump referred to it in an interview.

Trump was interviewed at 7AM on Fox & Friends on the day Indiana voters went to the polls. He was asked if he thought Cruz's father might sway Indiana's Evangelicals vote against him. Cruz's father, who is an evangelical preacher, had been campaigning on behalf of his son amongst Indiana's large Evangelical population, and saying rather extreme things about Trump and his supporters. He called Trump's supporters 'evil', and said Trump would cause the 'destruction' of America.

Fox and Friends aired a clip for Trump in which Cruz's father is seen telling Indiana voters that "Trump would destroy America if he was elected". Trump responded saying, *"I think it's a disgrace that he's allowed to do it, I think it's a disgrace that he's allowed to say it,"* but the way MSNBC's Steve Kornacki presented excerpts from the interview made it appear that what Trump said referred to JFK's assassination, when it actually referred to what Cruz's father had said about Trump.

Every hourly program on each network began with the same claim, expressed in progressively more extreme language as the day wore on. But each rendition had two things in common: each concealed that Trump was answering a question about Cruz's father, and that Cruz's father had attacked Trump while campaigning for his son in Indiana.

Kornacki was using the same tactic the Media had used to make it appear that what Trump said in jest on February 1, 2016—*"knock the crap out of him will you…I promise I'll pay your legal fees"*— in response to rumors that someone in the crowd at a rally was carrying a bag of tomatoes to throw at Trump, was said about an incident that occurred six weeks later, on March 8, 2016—when an elderly man punched a protester who gave the old man the middle finger as he was being escorted out of a stadium, and Trump wasn't even in the stadium as he had left.

The four o'clock programs on CNN and MSNBC saw the most vicious attacks on Trump: it was the news media's last chance before the polls closed in Indiana. CNN's shrill-voiced Tapper introduced Cruz diatribe by characterizing it as an understandable response to the vicious attacks Trump had made on Cruz's family, and linked it to the earlier Enquirer article accusing Cruz of infidelity that Rubio allies had pushed and Trump had nothing to do with, and had publicly said he hoped it was untrue.

The appearance of objectivity in which Chris Hayes tried to shroud his attack bordered on caricature. He first aired Cruz's entire diatribe against Trump with critical commentary, and his own surprise about its timing:

"What I can't understand is why he left it so late. Why didn't he say it before?" Hayes said.

The answer, of course, was that an earlier attack would have given Trump an opportunity to respond—and respond before crowds of tens of thousands of people. But Hayes didn't consider that explanation, and moved on to, ostensibly, the other side's point of view:

"And now for a reaction from the Trump camp we go to Katy Tur."

Katy Tur? She was going to give the reaction from the Trump campaign without even speaking to anyone from the Trump campaign? What Katy Tur presented wasn't the reaction of the Trump camp, but her own take on Cruz's diatribe—only she made it sound as if she were presenting facts, not her personal opinions, as she is always wont to do.

Tur described Cruz's diatribe as understandable, because it must be very hard to deal with a 'truth-challenged' opponent like Trump who kept repeating the same false statements even after their falsity was pointed out to him. She then catalogued the Media's every fabrication about Trump, and as she did, caught herself in a lie that she corrected while she was still speaking on the air:

"Like Muslims celebrating on 9/11 which no one saw....I mean thousands celebrating that no one saw...."

The news media's original false report—that no one had celebrated the fall of the World Trade Center on 9/11— had evidently imprinted itself in Katy Tur's memory, and she forgot the 'pivot' the news media used to obfuscate its false report—that no one saw *thousands* of people celebrate the fall of the World Trade Center on 9/11. That was just a rhetorical flourish Trump used once at a rally, but to Katy Tur like all the partisan reporters in the news media, it was a lie by a 'truth-challenged' candidate.

CHAPTER 30

It's All Over Now, Baby Blue

• • •

ALL THAT ENORMOUS EFFORT—IT WAS for naught. Hosiers didn't listen to Cruz: as soon as all the polls closed, the networks declared Trump the winner of the Indiana primary. The last firewall against him had collapsed.

Trump got over 50% of the vote—something pundits like Karl Rove told everyone wouldn't happen once it was a two-man race. He was wrong; they were all wrong. It wasn't even close. Trump won the Indiana primary by 16 points. He tweeted, THANK YOU INDIANA, as he had done to every state that voted for him.

Cruz spoke first. Everyone was wondering what he would do as he spoke in lofty generalities about America and the Constitution, and then the news was splashed across the television screen as he was speaking:

"Cruz will drop out of the race tonight."

A few minutes later Cruz confirmed that he was suspending his campaign. Katy Tur and others covering the Trump campaign tweeted and retweeted video clips showing the Trump camp quietly celebrating and hugging each other, on hearing the news. One felt the hugs for Corey Lewandowski were particularly emotional and well deserved. Then came the news the Trump camp probably most wanted to hear: Reince Priebus, the RNC chairman, declared Trump the Republican Party's presumptive nominee, and said it was time to unite the party behind him.

It was over. Cruz and the SuperPacs had spent $5.3 million dollars in negative advertisements against Trump in Indiana: Trump spent only $963,000. Overall, his opponents and their SuperPacs had spent $75.7 million on 64,000 negative advertisements attacking Trump. It didn't work. None of it worked. What everyone had confidently predicted wouldn't happen just happened. And some. Trump had got more votes in the primaries than any other Republican presidential candidate in history—more than Eisenhower, more than Nixon, more than even Reagan—and there were still nine primaries left.

One couldn't help feel that something momentous had happened, and that it was something good. There was optimism in the air. It was best captured by Bobby Knight—it hit a cord to hear a tough guy express such affection as only a tough guy could:

"I was very selective in picking my players," Knight began, and then, looking the crowd straight in the eye, said:

"but I can tell you that sumabitch could play for me."

The next day John Kasich suspended his campaign. It was over. Only formalities remained, but MSNBC's Andrea Mitchell could still only bring herself to call Trump the 'likely', not the 'presumptive' nominee. It was all just too much for her.

PART IV

The Denouement

• • •

CHAPTER 31

The Aftermath

• • •

To have doubted one's own first principles
is the mark of a civilized man.

OLIVER WENDELL HOLMES

TRUMP'S VICTORY BROUGHT NO RESPITE from the Media's baneful attacks. Undeterred by their hopelessly wrong primary predictions, the news media redoubled their attacks, and confidently predicted that Trump would be defeated in the general election, dismissing the significance of his primary victory with, *"what works in the primaries doesn't work in the general election"*.

"You can't win a general election without uniting the party": MSNBC's Chuck Todd was constantly telling viewers that on the air, and reviewed historical precedents to prove it. Trump would not be able to unite the Republican party, he predicted, and that was the narrative the cable news networks flooded the airways with for the next month, as everyone waited for the primaries to be formally concluded.

The House Speaker, Paul Ryan, at first declined to endorse Trump, fueling the disunity narrative, especially as the night following the

Indiana primary, Mitch McConnell, the Senate Majority Leader, said he would endorse Trump. But Ryan's dismissed McConnell's endorsement with

"saying we're unified doesn't in and of itself, unify us".

What it took to unify the party, Ryan, said, was

"taking the principles that we all believe in, showing that there's a dedication to those, and running a principles campaign that Republicans can be proud about, and that can actually appeal to a majority of Americans".

When asked by CNN's Jake Tapper if Ryan was saying that he couldn't support or endorse Trump right now, Ryan replied:

"Yes, I am basically saying that. Look, I'm — you know, I thought about this two days ago. I thought actually this was going to go to June 7th at the very least, probably to a convention. And so this is all pretty new for us. But at this point, I think that he needs do more to unify this party to bring all wings of the Republican Party together, and then to go forward and to appeal to all Americans and every walk of life, every background, a majority of independents and discerning Democrats. And so, you know, I think conservatives want to know, does he share our values and our principles on limited government, the proper role of the executive, adherence to the Constitution. There are a lot of questions that conservatives, I think, are going to want answers to, myself included. And I want to be a part of this unifying process. I want to help unify this party. But we have to unify it, I think, for us to be successful."

Tapper badgered Ryan, played him excerpts from Mitt Romney speech denouncing Trump, and repeatedly pressed him with questions about the possibility of uniting the party and beating Hillary Clinton that were hard to answer in the affirmative without seeming to contradict himself, but Ryan eventually said, to Tapper's visible disappointment,

> *"Just so you know, Jake, we're not there right now. We're not there right now. Yes, I think it's possible. But we're not there right now. And I think it is possible, and we better get on with it. But I think we just need to be honest with each other about these things, and look, I think, yes, I think we can beat Hillary Clinton. Are you kidding me? So yes, I think it's possible. And it needs to be possible because so much is at stake."*

The news media persisted with the disunity theme. They interviewed Trump's former opponents like Jeb Bush and Lindsay Graham, and repeatedly re-aired their declamations not to vote for Trump. Conservative operatives and Never Trump activists like Eric Erickson, who vowed to leave the party if Trump was nominated, were also repeatedly interviewed, and prominent Republicans canvassed about their intentions to attend the Convention. The Bushes, John McCain, Mitt Romney, and several Republican Senators up for re-election, like New Hampshire Senator Kelly Ayotte, all said they would not attend the Republican National Convention. Not Good.

The themes, *'Trump couldn't unite the Republican Party'* and *'Trump couldn't win a general election against Hillary Clinton'*, were bolstered with poll results showing that Trump had high negatives among women and minorities, and a CNN poll that had him losing to Hillary Clinton nationally by 13 points. Could Trump unite the party? Would a third party candidate emerge? Would Trump change his positions or act more presidential? These were the questions pundits were repeatedly asked.

Then MSNBS's Ari Melber tried unsuccessfully to manufacture a new story with which to disparage Trump: was his claim to have self-funded his campaign a hoax? Trump had lent money to his campaign, but could later pay himself back from money he raised after the Convention, Melber suggested. He acknowledged that Trump had categorically stated that he would not seek to be repaid for the money he'd spent, but Melber said he would be keeping a close eye on that—implying that he didn't believe Trump—but he still couldn't get any traction with his concocted narrative.

All the while, Clinton was bombarding the airwaves with negative advertisements about Trump, but Trump hadn't aired a single advertisement about Clinton. Clinton was also raising huge amounts of money, while he was raising none. Was his campaign in trouble? If all you read were Katy Tur's tweets you'd think Trump was about to give it all up.

The answer came in less than two weeks, when the polls were telling a very different story: Clinton's double digit lead in national polls had vanished, and the polls had her tied with Trump in the key battleground states of Florida and Pennsylvania, and losing to Trump in Ohio. So the Media changed tack.

There was first a discredited story in the *New York Times* about Trump's supposed mistreatment of women, but the women whom Trump was alleged to have abused themselves denied the allegations, and the story fizzled. The Times, not Trump ended up with egg on its face for yet again reporting unverified facts.

Then the news media turned its attention on Never Trump activists' attempts to get someone to run as a third party candidate against Trump. Mitt Romney said, categorically, that he would not run as a third party candidate, but then Bill Kristol tweeted that he had found a strong candidate, who was interested in running against Trump: David French, an Iraq veteran who no one had ever heard of—Kristol knew him because French was a staff writer for *National Review*.

Then Trump's supporters were attacked at a rally in San Diego on the Friday before the last primaries. The event was insufficiently policed, and Trump supporters were brutally attacked, American flags burned, and Mexican flags waived. One woman who supported Trump was pelted with eggs. This time it was too much even for the left to take, and Katy Tur tweeted, "*This is awful.*" This time everyone on the left except for the Mayor of San Diego, condemned the violence and the rioters, and not Trump—but the Mayor held Trump responsible, on a logic he did not express and no one could divine.

The final attack on Trump came the week before the last primaries. Trump was attacked as racist for saying that U.S. District Court Judge Gonzalo Curiel, who was presiding over two of the three law suits filed against Trump University in federal court in San Diego, was biased against him. This time the attack was significant because two of the states voting on June 7—California and New Mexico—had very large Hispanic populations.

Trump concluded that Judge Curiel could not be impartial towards him, given that Trump wanted to build a wall between the U.S. and Mexico, because the judge had expressed pride in his Mexican heritage, and was a member of the La Raza Lawyers of California, which is a special interest group, providing pro bono representation to Mexicans, and advocating for 'path to citizenship' and 'reduced deportations'. Wikipedia explains that La Raza

"translates as 'The Race'…having the meaning of 'race, ethnicity; breed, strain, lineage'. The term expresses ethnic or racial pride…"

Trump's opponents accused Trump and his supporters of falsely linking La Raza Lawyers of California to the left-wing activist group, the National Council of La Raza (NCLR), which Wikipedia describes as

"America's largest Latino advocacy organization. It advocates in favor of progressive immigration policies, including a path to citizenship and reduced deportations."

But if there's no connection, why did the lawyer association not call itself the Hispanic Lawyers of California or Latino Lawyers of California? Why did it call itself La Raza Lawyers of California, and why does it allow NCLR to advertise on its website? The only reasonable explanation is that the group supports and advocates for the same positions as NCLR.

Jake Tapper's predictable response was to label Trump a racist during an interview—the most remarkable aspect of which was that Trump agreed to the interview in the first place, given how Tapper had branded Trump a racist three months earlier by falsely claiming that Trump had failed to denounce the KKK. Tapper's interview illustrated that politicians cannot express opinions journalists disagree, even if they are rationally based, without being demonized and having their motives impugned. Tapper's position was that it is not rational but racist to attribute bias to a person's ethnic heritage: it was 'fine' for Trump to criticize the judge's decision, Tapper said, but not question his impartiality based on his heritage: that was racist, Tapper declared.

If so, that makes Supreme Court Justice Sonia Sotomayor also a racist, because in 2001 she expressly said in a speech at the University of California-Berkley that her gender and Latina heritage could be expected to influence her judicial decisions—she could not say how, but hoped in a good way:

"Whether born from experience or inherent physiological or cultural differences, a possibility I abhor less or discount less than my colleague Judge Cedarbaum, **our gender and national origins may and will make a difference in our judging.** *Justice O'Connor has often been cited as saying that a wise old man and wise old woman will reach the same conclusion in deciding cases. I am not so sure Justice O'Connor is the author of that line since Professor Resnik attributes that line to Supreme Court Justice Coyle. I am also not so sure that I agree with the statement."*[96] *(Boldface added)*

"Hence, one must accept the proposition that a difference there will be by the presence of women and people of color on the bench. **Personal experiences affect the facts that judges choose to**

---

96 http://www.berkeley.edu/news/media/releases/2009/05/26_sotomayor.shtml, ¶ 21

*see. My hope is that I will take the good from my experiences and extrapolate them further into areas with which I am unfamiliar. **I simply do not know exactly what that difference will be in my judging. But I accept there will be some based on my gender and my Latina heritage.**[97]* (Boldface added)

The left wing media tried quickly and zealously to change the meaning of what Justice Sotomayor said by citing to a different portion of her speech,[98] but everyone knows, and Justice Sotomayor was simply honest enough to admit it, that a judge's experiences, personal preferences and outlook will affect his or her decisions of any but the simples, black letter questions of law. If it were otherwise, there would not be such fierce fights in the Senate over nominations to the Supreme Court.

---

97 Id., ¶ 23
98 Id., ¶ 24; http://www.snopes.com/sonia-sotomayor-speech-donald-trump/

CHAPTER 32

Events, Dear Boy

• • •

Remember, one lie does not cost you
one truth but the truth.

<small>CHRISTIAN HEBBEL</small>

WHEN HAROLD MACMILLAN BECAME PRIME Minister of Great Britain in January, 1957 after Sir Anthony Eden resigned in the wake of the Suez crisis, a young journalist asked Macmillan what he thought would shape his premiership.

"*Events, dear boy, events,*" Macmillan replied.

And events—terrorists attacks in the U.S. and abroad, assassinations of American police officers, the results of the FB investigation into Hillary Clinton's emails— as much as the election preoccupied the nation between the last primaries on June 7, 2016 and the start of the Republican National Convention on July 18, 2016.

On June 12ᵗʰ, five days after the last primaries, 49 people were killed and 53 wounded in an ISIS-inspired attack inside a gay night-club in Orlando, Florida, by Omar Mateen, a 29-year old,

American-born Muslim of Afghan parents, using a semi-automatic rifle. Meteen's father, Seddique, supported the Taliban, and hosts *'Durand Jirga Show'*, a program that airs on a California-based satellite Afghan TV station and caters to ethnic Pashtun Afghans living in the U.S. and Europe, and that is "full of anti-U.S. rhetoric".[99] Two months later, he appeared at a Hillary Clinton rally in Florida—at the invitation of the Democrat Party, he said. The National and Florida Democrat parties denied inviting Mateen. Hillary Clinton did not distance herself from him at least, not at first.

The next day, a police chief in Paris and his partner were stabbed to death by a man claiming allegiance to the Islamic State.[100]

Three days later, on June 28, 2016, the first attack tied to the Islamic State occurred in Malaysia, when eight people were injured in a night club by a grenade. The next day, three suicide bombers killed at least 41 people and injured dozens more at Ataturk Airport in Istanbul, Turkey.[101]

On Saturday of the July 4th weekend, three Americans were among the 22 people killed in a cafe in Dhaka, the capital of Bangladesh, by ISIS operatives wielding blades and guns,[102] and at least 200 people were killed the same day by a truck bomb in Baghdad, for which ISIS claimed responsibility.[103]

---

99 http://www.cbsnews.com/news/orlando-shooting-omar-mateen-father-seddique-mateen-taliban-god-punish-gays/

100 https://www.theguardian.com/world/2016/jun/13/french-policeman-stabbed-death-paris

101 http://www.usatoday.com/story/news/2016/06/28/reports-least-10-dead-blast-istanbul-airport/86481174/

102 http://www.nbcnews.com/news/world/bangladesh-attack-u-s-citizen-among-20-foreigners-killed-dhaka-n602866

103 http://www.cnn.com/2016/07/02/middleeast/baghdad-car-bombs/

The same day as these massacres were taking place, it was reported that the FBI had interviewed Hillary Clinton. Then, at eleven o'clock, immediately after the long July 4th weekend, the Director of the FBI, James Comey, convened a press conference at very short notice—without informing the press what it would be about—and reported the findings of the FBI's investigation into Hillary Clinton's emails and use of a private server, without taking any questions.

Comey first detailed the investigation the FBI had conducted, and then said, *"Now let me tell you what we found"*. [104]

Comey stated that although there was no evidence of intentional wrongdoing,

> *"there is evidence that they were extremely careless in their handling of very sensitive, highly classified information, and that any reasonable person in Secretary Clinton's position, or in the position of those government employees with whom she was corresponding about these matters, should have known that an unclassified system was no place for that conversation. None of these e-mails should have been on any kind of unclassified system."* [105]

This finding proved that Hillary Clinton's repeated claim that her use of the server was authorized was not true.

> *"I have so far used the singular term, "e-mail server," in describing the referral that began our investigation. It turns out to have*

104 https://www.fbi.gov/news/pressrel/press-releases/statement-by-fbi-director-james-b-comey-on-the-investigation-of-secretary-hillary-clinton2019s-use-of-a-personal-e-mail-system
105 Id.

been more complicated than that. Secretary Clinton used several different servers and administrators of those servers during her four years at the State Department, and used numerous mobile devices to view and send e-mail on that personal domain," Comey continued.

This revelation gave the lie to Clinton's claim that she only used one cell phone while she was Secretary of State, and to the explanation Clinton gave for using a private server in the first place— that she thought it would be "easier," "better," "simpler" and more convenient for her to *"carry just one device for my work and for my personal emails instead of two".*

"Looking back, it would've been better for me to use two separate phones and two email accounts. I thought using one device would be simpler and, obviously, it hasn't worked out that way," she had told the public.[106]

Comey said that of the 30,000 emails Clinton turned over to the State Department, the 'owning agency' determined that

"52 email chains contain classified information at the time they were sent or received";
> *"8 chains contained information that was '**Top Secret**"*;
> *"36chains contained '**Secret**' information"*; and
> *"8 chains contained '**Confidential**' information."*[107]
(Boldface added).

---

106 http://abcnews.go.com/Politics/hillary-clinton-phones-secretary-state-now/story?id=29535505
107 Id.

These findings proved that what Hillary Clinton had repeatedly told the public—*"I never sent or received any classified information"*—was also untrue.

Comey said that the FBI discovered *"several thousand work-related e-mails that were not in the group of 30,000 that were returned by Secretary Clinton to State in 2014"*—and that there were likely many more work-related emails that the FBI could not recover—proving that Hillary Clinton's repeated assurances to the public that she had turned over all work-related emails to the State Department was not true.

Among the work-related emails the FBI discovered were not turned over to the State Department, 3 were classified at the time they were sent or received—*"one at the 'Secret' level and two at the 'Confidential' level"*— Comey said.[108]

The FBI determined from the interviews it had conducted that Hillary Clinton's lawyers had not actually read any of the emails, and had used search terms to identify which emails were work-related and which were not. This finding proved that Hillary Clinton had again not told the truth when she told the public and Congress that in an abundance of caution, her lawyers had carefully read the emails and were overly inclusive in what they turned over to the State Department.

Finally, Comey said that although

"only a very small number of the e-mails containing classified information bore markings indicating the presence of classified

---

108 Id.

information…even if information is not marked 'classified' in an e-mail, participants who know or should know that the subject matter is classified are still obligated to protect it."[109]

Comey's statement confirmed what Governor Christie and other Clinton critics had been saying. Moreover, three emails were marked as classified *when they were sent or received*, which meant that the modified representation Clinton was making to the public about the emails—that none of the emails she sent or received were *marked* as classified—was also not true.

Comey said that although the FBI found no evidence that Clinton's server had been hacked, but concluded that it *"would be highly unlikely to see such evidence"*, and that it was possible that Clinton's private server was hacked given that:

* the private commercial e-mail accounts of people whom Clinton was in regular contact with from her private server was hacked;
* her use of a personal e-mail domain was known *"by a large number of people and readily apparent"*; and
* Clinton used her personal e-mail extensively outside the U.S., and sent and received work-related e-mails *"in the territory of sophisticated adversaries"*.

Having catalogued the FBI's findings, Comey went on to explain that he was recommending to the Attorney General that no charges be brought against Hillary Clinton, and explained why:

---

109 http://abcnews.go.com/Politics/hillary-clinton-phones-secretary-state-now/story?id=29535505

"We cannot find a case that would support bringing criminal charges on these facts," Comey said. *"All the cases prosecuted involved some combination of: clearly intentional and willful mishandling of classified information; or vast quantities of materials exposed in such a way as to support an inference of intentional misconduct; or indications of disloyalty to the United States; or efforts to obstruct justice. "We do not see those things here,"* he concluded.[110]

There was relief on the political left, uproar on the right, with a majority of the public s disagreeing with the decision not to indict Clinton. In a Rasmussen poll taken the night Comey announced that he would not recommend indicting Hillary Clinton, 63% of voters not affiliated with either major political party disagreed with the decision;[111] a week after Comey's announcement, an ABC/Washington Post poll found that 56% of likely voters disagreed with the decision not to indict Clinton.[112]

The decision was also harshly criticized by legal commentators. They said that the FBI was effectively rewriting the law, because it required only gross negligence to violate the applicable statute, 18 U.S.C. § 793(f), and there is no "intent" requirement. Because the FBI found that Clinton had been *'extremely careless'*, which means the same thing as gross negligence, the FBI found that she had violated the applicable section of the Penal Code. Moreover, Clinton had acted with intent, many critics pointed out, because she intended to bypass government regulation: it didn't happen by accident.

---

110 http://abcnews.go.com/Politics/hillary-clinton-phones-secretary-state-now/story?id=29535505
111 http://www.rasmussenreports.com/public_content/politics/general_politics/july_2016/most_disagree_with_decision_not_to_indict_clinton
112 http://time.com/4400757/hillary-clinton-fbi-james-comey-poll/

Two days later, Comey appeared before the House Oversight and Government Reform Committee and was grilled by Republicans about his decision. The hearing achieved two things: (1) it created a clear record that Clinton had repeatedly lied to the public about her emails; and (2) the FBI received a referral to investigate whether Clinton had lied to Congress about her emails during her testimony about Benghazi, which Comey, to the surprise of many, said he needed to investigate that question.

Later on the day that Comey testified before Congress, the focus of public attention changed after Micah Xavier Johnson, a 25-year old, African-American army reserve veteran, ambushed and killed five police officers and injured seven others in Dallas Texas. It happened at the end of a peaceful Black Lives Matter-organized protest condemning the police shooting of two black men— Alton Sterling in Baton Rouge, Louisiana, and Philando Castile in St. Anthony, Minnesota— by white police officers.

During two hours of negotiations before he was killed by a robot-delivered bomb, Johnson told police that he wanted to exterminate white people, especially white police officers. Police found bomb making equipment in Johnson's apartment, and that he had practiced detonating them, leading police to believe that Johnson was planning wider attacks. Although not linked to ISIS, Johnson was linked to three hate groups: the New Black Panther Party, the Nation of Islam, and the Black Riders Liberation Party.

A week later, on July 14, 2016, the public's attention reverted back to Islamic terrorism and Europe, after a 31-year old Tunisian resident of France, Mohamed Lahouaiej-Bouhlel, drove a 19-ton cargo truck into crowds celebrating Bastille Day on the Promenade des

Anglais in Nice, France, killing 84 people and injuring 303. ISIS later claimed the attack was executed *"in response to calls to target citizens of coalition nations which fight the Islamic State"*.[113] French prosecutors said Lahouaiej-Bouhlel had been planning the attack for some time, and had five accomplices who were in custody. It brought the total number of people killed by the Islamic State in 2016 outside of Iraq and Syria to more than 1,200, the *New York Times* reported.[114] Almost half the attacks targeted Westerners.

On the day the Republican Convention started, three police officers were assassinated in Baton Rouge, Louisiana, and the next day a 17-year old Afghan refugee attacked and seriously injured three people with an axe on a train in Germany. ISIS issued the following statement, claiming responsibility for the attack:

> *"The perpetrator of the stabbing attack in Germany was one of the fighters of the Islamic State and carried out the operation in answer to the calls to target the countries of the coalition fighting the Islamic State."*[115]

These events set the stage for the Republican Convention at which riots and violence were anticipated but never materialized thanks to superb police organization that prevented anyone from getting closer than four blocks from the convention center.

---

113 Thomas Joscelyn, The Long War Journal, 16 July 2016

114 http://www.nytimes.com/interactive/2016/03/25/world/map-isis-attacks-around-the-world.html?_r=0

115 http://www.telegraph.co.uk/news/2016/07/18/german-train-axe-attack-many-injured/

CHAPTER 33

Trump Triumphant: the Republican National Convention

• • •

If you can trust yourself when all men doubt you,
But make allowance for their doubting too;

RUDYARD KIPLING

THE REPUBLICAN NATIONAL CONVENTION OPENED in Cleveland, Ohio, on Monday, July 18, 2016. True to form, Trump's opponents described it as a *'train wreck'*, a *'fiasco'*, a *'carnival'*, a *'nuclear dumpster fire'*.[116] In the build-up to the Convention, the news media saturated the airwaves with speculation about the likely protests and violence at Convention, and the chaos Cruz supporters and Never Trump delegates would likely create on the convention floor.

None of their speculations materialized. The growing unity in the Conference Hall was palpable, and could be heard in the frequent roars of TRUMP-TRUMP-TRUMP with which the delegates

---

116 http://time.com/4418423/donald-trump-republican-convention-hillary-clinton/?xid=newsletter-brief

interrupted the speeches. Out on the streets, the atmosphere was best capture by a Cleveland police officer playing table tennis with a protester on the third day of the Convention.

The week prior to the convention, a motion by Cruz supporters to change the convention rules was defeated by a vote of 87 to 12. A small group of Never Trump delegates and Cruz supporters led by Utah Sen. Mike Lee continued their efforts to change the convention rules, and forced a voice vote on the Convention floor on Monday, before the Convention was formally opened. A small skirmish lasting about 30-minute developed after they were defeated for a second time that several news outlets described as 'chaos erupting on the GOP convention floor',[117] but no one else seemed to notice.

Despite the hateful attacks on Trump as a racist, something he had never been called before he ran for president, many members of the African-American and Latino communities attended the Convention, and Cleveland-area pastor Darrell Scott, Milwaukee County Sheriff David Clarke, and pastor Mark Burns of South Carolina, gave electrifying speeches. Pastor Burns denounced Hillary Clinton and the Democrats for

"focusing on the color that divides us instead of the colors that unite us"

to roars of approval from the crowd. But Trump's children stole the show. They infused the Convention with a positive energy so infectious that even the news media's relentless carping and refusal to give the Trumps their due could not diminish it.

---

117 http://www.politico.com/story/2016/07/never-trump-delegates-have-support-needed-to-force-rules-vote-225716

A member of Trump's immediate family spoke each day, starting with Trump's wife, Melania, who spoke on the first day. She was preceded by New York's former mayor, Rudi Giuliani, who gave a fiery defense of Donald Trump, a friend of 30 years, that was reminiscent of Mark Anthony's peroration at Caesar's funeral.[118]

Giuliani started by thanking the police

"For protecting us, black, white, Latino… of every race, every color, every creed, every sexual orientation. When they come to save your life they don't ask whether you are Black or white. They just come to save you," he roared.

"We also reach out our arms in understanding and compassion to those who have lost loved ones because of police shootings: some justified, some unjustified," he continued. *"Those that are unjustified must be punished. Those that are justified we much apologize to."*

"It's time to make America safe again; it's time to make American O-N-E again. What happened to there is no white America, there is no black America, there is only AMERICA? What happened to it. Where did it go?" he roared again, beseeching the audience for an answer, reminding it of what Barak Obama had said when he first ran for President in 2008.

Then, turning his attention to his friend, Donald Trump, Giuliani told the crowd,

"This is a man with a big heart. Every time New York suffered a tragedy, Donald Trump was there to help. He's not going to like

---

118 William Shakespeare, Julius Caesar, Act III, Sc. II

my telling you this, but he did it anonymously. When police officers were shot, when firemen were hurt, when people were in trouble, he came forward to help, and he asked not to be mentioned."

"Well, I am going to break my promise to him. I am going to mention it: this is a man with a big heart who loves people—all people—from the top to the bottom, from the middle to the side. I am telling you this because I am sick and tired of the defamation of Donald Trump by the Media and the Clinton campaign. I am sick and tired of it. This is a good man, and America should be tired of their vicious, nasty campaign."

It was a stirring speech. Giuliani not only said what needed to be said, but said it from the bottom of his heart, and it was obvious that meant every word he said. It was baleful that the news media found an excuse to ignore it—plagiarism! The news media accused not Giuliani but Melania Trump, whose speech followed Giuliani's, of plagiarizing the speech Michelle Obama gave to the Democrat Convention in 2008, and talked about practically nothing else for the next two days.

Well, that's not quite accurate. The news media didn't have the temerity to accuse Melania: they would never have the guts to take her on. They accused her speech writer, and bayed for the person's blood the whole of the next day. They even sucked RNC chairman, Reince Priebus, into saying that it seemed reasonable to him that someone should be 'fired'.

Melania Trump gave a remarkable speech, and in its immediate aftermath most of the news media were agog, and fawned over it and her. Brit Hume called it fabulous, Mike Wallace called her *"drop dead gorgeous*"—but spared us the breathless, heavy breathing with which Chris Mathews spoke about Melania as she followed her husband to the microphone after Trump won the Indiana primary, not realizing that his microphone was still on.

Melania delivered the speech fluently in English, the last of the five languages she learned to speak. She was poised, self-assured, relaxed. She looked stunningly beautiful in the simple white dress she wore, and exuded style and elegance. She was unpretentious: what she said was sincere, interesting, and relevant. But the news media tried to diminish the success of the occasion by denouncing the speech as plagiarized.

> "*From a young age, my parents impressed on me the values that you work hard for what you want in life, that your word is your bond and you do what you say and keep your promise, that you treat people with respect. They taught and showed me values and morals in their daily lives. That is a lesson that I continue to pass along to our son. And we need to pass those lessons on to the many generations to follow. Because we want our children in this nation to know that the only limit to your achievements is the strength of your dreams and your willingness to work for them.*"

That was the part of Melania's speech the news media said was plagiarized from Michelle Obama.[119] Real plagiarism is, of course, a deliberate attempt to take credit for an original idea, or the origi-

---

119 "*And Barack and I were raised with so many of the same values: that you work hard for what you want in life; that your word is your bond and you do what you say you're going to do; that you treat people with dignity and respect, even if you don't know them, and even if you don't agree with them. And Barack and I set out to build lives guided by these values, and to pass them on to the next generation. Because we want our children — and all children in this nation — to know that the only limit to the height of your achievements is the reach of your dreams and your willingness to work for them.*"

nal expression of an idea, by stealing it from someone else—like the following, very original passage from a speech Governor Patrick Duvall gave during the 2006 gubernatorial race in Massachusetts that Obama plagiarized in 2008, when he first ran for President:

> *"'We hold these truths to be self-evident, that all men are created equal'-just words. Just words. 'We have nothing to fear but fear itself'-just words. 'Ask not what your country can do for you, ask what you can do for your country'-just words. 'I have a dream'-just words?"*[120]

Or like the following, original and emotionally stirring passage from a speech Neil Kinnock gave during the 1987 UK election that Biden famously plagiarized, and was forced him to quit the 1988 presidential race over, after he was caught doing it:

> *"Why am I the first Kinnock in a thousand generations to be able to get to university? Was it because our predecessors were thick? Does anybody really think that they didn't get what we had because they didn't have the talent or the strength or the endurance or the commitment? Of course not. It was because there was no platform upon which they could stand."*[121]

Melania Trump didn't do anything like what Obama and Biden had done. Nor did the offending passage contain the kind of original

---

120 Obama plagiarized the idea and part of Duvall's speech, saying to his audience: *"Don't tell me words don't matter! 'I have a dream.' Just words. 'We hold these truths to be self-evident, that all men are created equal.' Just words. 'We have nothing to fear but fear itself.' Just words, just speeches?"*

121 http://www.telegraph.co.uk/news/worldnews/barackobama/2607505/Joe-Biden-plagiarised-Neil-Kinnock-speech.html Worse still, was the disclosure that in 1965, during his first year at Syracuse University Law School, Biden initially received an "F" in an introductory class on legal methodology for writing a paper relying almost exclusively on a Fordham Law Review article, which he had cited only once. *E. J. Dionne, The New York Times, September 18, 1987.*

ideas or sentiments that Obama and Biden stole from others. But the Media had a field day, and beat the plagiarism horse to death for the next two days, drowning out news about the other speeches, using it to excoriate the Trump campaign for its lack of professionalism, demanding that the person responsible to be fired.

The baying stopped after Meredith McIver, who helped Melania write the speech, tendered her resignation to Trump in a letter that was made public on the third day of the Convention:

"In working with Melania Trump on her recent First Lady speech," she wrote, *"we discussed many people who inspired her and messages she wanted to share with the American people. A person she has always liked is Michelle Obama. Over the phone, she read me some passages from Mrs. Obama's speech as examples. I wrote them down and later included some of the phrasing in the draft that ultimately became the final speech. I did not check Mrs. Obama's speeches. This was my mistake, and I feel terrible for the chaos I have caused Melania and the Trumps, as well as to Mrs. Obama. No harm was meant."*

"Yesterday, I offered my resignation to Mr. Trump and the Trump family, but they rejected it. Mr. Trump told me that people make mistakes and that we learn and grow from these experiences."

"I asked to put out this statement," she added, *"because I did not like the way this was distracting from Mr. Trump's historic campaign for President, and Melania's beautiful message and presentation. I apologize for the confusion and hysteria my mistake has caused."*

The letter silenced the news media, and made the likes of Joe Scarborough look so small and vulgar and mean-spirited, just as they looked baying for blood after Michelle Fields made her contrived allegations against Corey Lewandowski.

Two of Trump's children spoke on the second day. Tiffany, Trump's 22-year old youngest daughter, who had just graduated from the University of Pennsylvania, did not look the least bit nervous as she talked about her father, describing him as a doting dad who scribbled notes on her school report card.

Donald Jr. followed Tiffany, and his speech stole the show. Many of the headlines the next day read: "A Political Star is Born". Frank Luntz convened a focus group of nineteen undecided voters, all of whom said the speech *'blew them away'* and sixteen of them said it convinced them to vote for Trump.

"This has never happened before," Luntz said, looking genuinely bewildered after counting the raised hands. But the speech's brilliance stuck in the craw of many NBC/MSNBC reporters. All Rachel Maddow could bring herself to say about it was, *"he knows how to read a teleprompter"*.

The news media avoided discussing Donald Jr.'s speech by focusing on Chris Christie's and Ben Carson's speeches instead, denouncing both their attacks on Hillary Clinton as "over the top'. Chris Christie conducted a faux prosecution of Hillary Clinton:

"We're going to present the facts to you," Christie explained to his audience. *"You, tonight, sitting as a jury of her peers, both in this hall and in your living rooms, around our nation. You see, since the Justice*

Department refuses to allow you to render a verdict, I'm going to present the case now, on the facts, against Hillary Rodham Clinton."

"Now, she was America's Chief Diplomat. So, let's look around the world at the violence and the danger, today, in every region that has been infected by her flawed judgment. But, I'm going to be specific so that you can render your verdict tonight on the basis of facts."

Christie then summarized the foreign policy decisions Clinton had made in several regions of the world—Nigeria, China, Syria, Russia, Cuba— and, after recounting facts of her decisions in each area, asked the audience:

"Guilty or not guilty?"
"Guilty!" was the audience's verdict on each charge.

Ben Carson told the audience that one of Hillary Clinton's heroes and mentors—the person she greatly admired and wrote her senior thesis about—was Saul Alinsky, a radical whose book, *Rules for Radicals*, was dedicated to Lucifer. But, he pointed out, that America's founding document,

"the Declaration of Independence talks about certain inalienable rights that come from our 'Creator'. This is a nation where the pledge of allegiance says 'Under God'. This is a nation where every coin in our pocked and every bill in our wallet says 'In God We Trust."

"So," he asked the audience, *"are we willing to elect someone as President who has as their role model someone who acknowledges Lucifer?"*

Calling Hillary Clinton Lucifer (which Carson never did) was denounced as 'over the top' by the news media the next day.

Eric Trump, who at the age of 22 set up a foundation to help St. Jude's Children's Research Hospital, gave a moving tribute to his father, describing him as his *'hero and best friend'*, and, looking straight into the camera, described who his father was running for:

> *"To the unemployed worker sitting at home watching me right now, wondering how you're going to make the next mortgage payment or rent payment—my father is running for you."*

> *"The single mothers, families with special needs children, middle class families no longer able to afford medical benefit sufficient to meet their needs—my father is running for you."*

He ended by urging the audience

> *"To vote for the candidate who is running for the right reasons… Who can't be bought, sold, purchased, bribed, coerced, intimidated or steered from the path that is right and just and true."*

> *"Never have I been more proud to be a Trump. Never have I been more proud to be my father's son,"* he said, and then, turning towards him, said to his father,

> *"Dad, you've once again taught us by example. You are my hero, you are my best friend, and you are the next President of the United States."*

It was, as Americas like to say, 'a class act', a sharp contrast to the pompous ideologue who spoke before him: Ted Cruz—who delighted the news media and Hillary Clinton by not endorsing Trump. The news media tried to create a false reality about the Convention after Cruz's speech with the headlines:

"Republican Unity Façade Shattered"
"Attempt at Party Unity Falls Short"
"Party Unity Cracks"

In reality, Ted Cruz was booed, even by the Texas delegations, so loudly that many said the floor of the arena shook. The New York delegation shouted at Cruz to endorse Trump, and Cruz's wife had to be escorted out as the crowd had turned on her. In a CNN/ORC poll conducted after the speech, Ted Cruz's approval rating among Republicans fell by 50%.[122]

Cruz had badly misjudged the mood on the Convention floor: Trump had outsmarted him, but the news media just didn't get what had gone down. It was too busy mocking Trump and his campaign, calling them disorganized and unprofessional for not reviewing Cruz's speech, and allowing Cruz to speak without knowing if he would endorse Trump.

Joe Scarborough and his cronies couldn't help themselves: they patronized and lectured and hectored the Trump campaign about what professional campaigns do, asking rhetorically what competent campaign would allow someone to speak at a Convention who was

---

122 https://www.washingtonpost.com/news/the-fix/wp/2016/07/25/ted-cruzs-donald-trump-burn-may-have-backfired/

not going to endorse the nominee? You'd think that was pretty elementary, wouldn't you?

News media hacks were still trashing Trump and his campaign when they learned that Trump and his campaign *had* reviewed Cruz's speech, and knew that Cruz was not going to endorse Trump. The news media hacks fell silent: they couldn't figure it out: none of them—not even Karl Rove. All he could say was that Cruz and Trump had both made a mistake: Cruz for not endorsing Trump, and Trump for allowing Cruz to speak.

They still didn't get that one of Trump's greatest strengths is his ability to judge people: he inherited that from his mother. Trump read the mood of the Convention correctly: Cruz hadn't. As Trump had correctly said about Cruz, *"he's very intelligent, but he doesn't use his intelligence wisely"*.

Trump knew that Cruz could have been a thorn in his side throughout the general election because it was to Cruz's advantage for Trump to lose. Trump realized that. So, having taken the measure of the delegates, and the mood and energy on the Convention floor, Trump gave Cruz the rope to hang himself with. He outsmarted everyone, and ensured that Cruz would not be able to undermine him during the general election. The nosedive that Cruz's approval rating took after his speech confirmed it.

Trump was introduced by his daughter Invanka, the family member closest to Trump, and who Eric admitted in an interview "is the family princess". She had a remarkable stage presence. Her self-assured, dignified elegance was tinged with girlish charm, and she delivered mature and accurate observations about matters with confidence, yet the freshness of a young millennial.

Ivanka described her father as "color blind and gender neutral", who was interested only in talent, and promoted talented women in the Trump organization, and paid them as much or more than men. She outlined some of his policies. She spoke with conviction, and was convincing about the kind of man her father was.

Trump then gave a speech that his supporters described as the most effective acceptance speech in living memory,[123] one that even rivaled Ronald Reagan's.[124]

"I haven't seen the left this upset with a GOP speech since Ronald Reagan," Laura Ingraham declared.[125]

But it was not a speech one would have expected from a billionaire businessman, for he offered himself as the champion and voice of the underdogs in society, not of corporations or the wealthy and the privileged:

"America is a nation of believers, dreamers, and strivers that is being led by a group of censors, critics, and cynics," he said.

---

123 http://www.newsmax.com/Politics/Rudy-Giuliani-Trump-Acceptance-Speech-Praise/2016/07/22/id/740011/

124 http://video.foxnews.com/v/5045983002001/gingrich-grades-trumps-speech-rivals-reagan-at-his-peak/?#sp=show-clips

125 http://www.foxnews.com/opinion/2016/07/22/laura-ingraham-havent-seen-left-this-upset-with-gop-speech-since-ronald-reagan.html

"I have joined the political arena so that the powerful can no longer beat up on people that cannot defend themselves."[126]

"Every day I wake up determined to deliver for the people I have met all across this nation that have been neglected, ignored, and abandoned."

"I have visited the laid-off factory workers, and the communities crushed by our horrible and unfair trade deals. These are the forgotten men and women of our country. People who work hard but no longer have a voice. I AM YOUR VOICE," he told them.

Trump seemed to personally commit himself to ending the plight of young people in the inner cities, who had poor educational and job opportunities, and who were surrounded by crime and violence. His statements came across as sincere and heartfelt.

"This Administration has failed America's inner cities. It's failed them on education. It's failed them on jobs. It's failed them on crime. It's failed them in every way and on every level."

"When I am President, I will work to ensure that all of our kids are treated equally, and protected equally. Every action I take, I will ask myself: does this make life better for young Americans in Baltimore, Chicago, Detroit, Ferguson who have the same right to live out their dreams as any other child in America?"

But even more surprising were Trump's *ad lib* comments. First, he waved off shouts of *"Lock her up! Lock her up!"*, as a way of saying 'no'

---

126 http://www.politico.com/story/2016/07/full-transcript-donald-trump-nomination-acceptance-speech-at-rnc-225974#ixzz4FAqBiw00

to the crowd's demands for Hillary Clinton's incarceration, and said to the delegates, *"Let's defeat her"*.

Then Trump made the following astonishing statements about a topic Mitt Romney didn't even dare mention four years earlier.

"Only weeks ago in Orlando, Florida, 49 wonderful Americans were murdered by an Islamic terrorist. This time, the terrorist targeted our LGBTQ community," Trump said. *"As your President I will do everything in my power to protect our LGBTQ citizens from the violence and oppression of a hateful foreign ideology,"* he promised.

Trump paused after he made his promise, looked around at the crowd after the cheering had died down, and said off the cuff:

"And I have to say as a Republican, it is so nice to hear you cheering for what I just said."

This time, the roar of the crowd practically lifted the roof off the arena, leaving those in the news media who had demonized Trump scratching their heads, and looking at each other in bemusement, obviously wondering, *"what the hell's going on"*.

Predictably, Trump's detractors had nothing good to say about his speech, and called it "dark". President Obama characteristically set up the straw man, saying that according to Trump *"America was on the verge of collapse"*, and then proceeded to knock the straw man down.

"This idea that America is somehow on the verge of collapse, this vision of violence and chaos everywhere, doesn't really jibe with the

experience of most people. The fears conveyed just don't jibe with the facts," Obama said.

A few hours later, Americans learned that a terrorist had killed nine people in Munich, Germany, and left three of the injured fighting for their lives on critical life support.

Two days later a 21-year old Syrian refugee killed a woman near Stuttgart, Germany with a machete, and an ISIS suicide bomber killed more than 80 people in Kabul, Afghanistan.

A week later, an Islamic terrorist cut a Catholic priest's throat in a small town in Normandy, France, while the priest was saying mass.

Trump got a 6% bounce from the Convention—it was, apparently, the first time any candidate in either party got a bounce out of a convention since 2000[127]. Trump led Hillary Clinton by 3%-4% in a two-way match up in each of the four polls conducted over the weekend following the Convention. The statistician Nate Silver, who gave Trump a 20% chance of winning the general election in June, 2016, said on Monday after the Convention that Trump now had a 57.5% of winning the general election.

But the sense of euphoria did not last long.

---

127 http://www.outsidethebeltway.com/trump-leads-clinton-after-convention-bounce/

PART V

Why the News Media & Political Class Failed to Stop Trump

• • •

CHAPTER 34

Why the News Media Failed: Questions of Fact

• • •

If you can bear to hear the truth you've spoken
Twisted by knaves to make a trap for fools

Rudyard Kipling

Why couldn't the non-stop negative stories about Trump aired throughout the day, every day for a year by the news media kill his candidacy— if Trump really did call all Mexicans rapists, called women he didn't like slobs and pigs, mocked a disabled reporter and another reporter's periods, and he really was a liar, a racist, sexist, misogynist, anti-immigrant, and an anti-Muslim, xenophobic bigot, who incited violence at his rallies, as the media claimed? How is that possible?

The simple answer is that it isn't possible—and it didn't happen. Time and time again, the *gist* of what Trump said was proved true: the public saw through the media's attempt to distort what Trump had said and portray him to be what he is not, and didn't buy the media's version of Trump—and it all just backfired.

ILLEGAL IMMIGRATION

The news media's outcry against Trump started immediately after he announced his candidacy, and it was against his statements about illegal immigration, building a wall, and deporting illegal immigrants. The news media took what Trump said about *illegal* immigrant and applied it to *all* immigrants and Mexicans, and repeatedly denounced Trump as anti-immigrant and xenophobic, and accused him of calling all immigrants and Mexican rapists. It presumably thought no one would notice, but they did: the accusations were simply not true, and no matter how the news media's paid pundits tried to justify their disagreements with Trump's immigration policies they couldn't make the news media's false allegations about Trump true. To those who watched him interviewed over and over again by a hostile media, Trump just didn't come across as someone who hated people—Mexicans or immigrants or blacks or anyone else.

Trump's position on immigration was very straight forward: you can't have a country if you don't have borders, which means you have to control immigration, and stop illegal immigration. The gist of what Trump said about illegal immigrants was also true: they bring a lot of problems with them, not only drugs and crime, but socio-economic problems. They take blue collar-jobs from Americans, and they are a drain on resources by consuming services like education and health care without paying any taxes. They are what economists call 'free-riders' on 'public goods'.

The news media demonized Trump for these views and called them divisive: President Barak Obama periodically joined the chorus of Trump's critics. But there was a big problem with that—the news media was very well aware of it, and assiduously tried to conceal it from the public, but you can't hide in a twitter world. Someone remembered what Obama had said about the threat that illegal immigration posed to American blue collar jobs in the book he wrote in 2006, *Audacity of Hope*:

> *"There's no denying that many blacks share the anxiety of many whites about the* **wave of illegal immigrants flooding our Southern border.** *The number of immigrants added to the labor force every year is of a magnitude not seen in this country for over a century. If this huge influx of mostly low-skill workers provides some benefits to the economy overall,* **it also threatens to depress the wages of blue-collar Americans, and puts strains on an already overburdened safety-net.**"[128] (bold face added)

In an article that had the headline, '*Donald Trump's False Comments Connecting Mexican Immigrants and Crime*', Michelle Ye Hee Lee, a *Washington Post* fact-checker tried to give the lie to Trump's claim that *illegal immigration* is linked to crime by citing to statistics showing that the crime rate among *immigrants* is lower than among the native population—although reverts to the native population's rate among their children.[129] They hoped no one would notice the sleight of hand, but they did.[130]

MSNBC's Chuck Todd also denounced Trump's statements about illegal immigration, on *Meet the Press*, saying,

---

128 http://dailycaller.com/2014/11/16/shock-flashback-obama-says-illegal-immigration-hurts-blue-collar-americans-strains-welfare-video/

129 https://www.washingtonpost.com/news/fact-checker/wp/2015/07/08/donald-trumps-false-comments-connecting-mexican-immigrants-and-crime/

130 http://www.americanthinker.com/articles/2015/07/illegal_aliens_murder_at_a_much_higher_rate_than_us_citizens_do.html

"We couldn't find a single study that linked violent crime and immigration."[131]

But you can't get away with false statements like that in a twitter world. When asked why he had not reference the Government Accounting Office's 2011 *Criminal Alien Statistics* report,[132] an aide to Chuck Todd said, *"no comment"*, causing *Breitbart* to accuse NBC of covering up crime statistics for illegal immigrants.[133]

Estimating crime rates among illegal immigrants is fraught with methodological problems, which affords partisans the opportunity to accept or reject any estimated rate depending on whether the rate comports with their ideological views. But one thing remains clear: Trump was talking about *illegal* immigrants, not *all* immigrants, and those trying to discredit his views were not citing statistics liking crime and *illegal* immigration: they were citing crime rates applicable to *all* immigrants, legal as well as illegal. (*Legal* immigrants, unlike *illegal* ones, are screened, and those convicted of crimes in the past are denied entry, which may account for the lower crime rate in *first* generation *legal* immigrants).

Obama had himself recognized the problems illegal immigration poses, and promised to enact immigration reform when he first ran for President in 2008. He could have enacted immigration reforms during his first two years in office when the House and Senate were both Democrat, but he chose to enact Health Care reform—*'Obamacare'*— instead, and reneged on his promise to enact

---

131 http://www.breitbart.com/big-government/2015/07/20/no-comment-nbc-covers-up-evidence-of-immigration-crime-wave/

132 http://www.gao.gov/assets/320/316959.pdf

133 http://www.breitbart.com/big-government/2015/07/20/no-comment-nbc-covers-up-evidence-of-immigration-crime-wave/

immigration reform. In interview after interview, Trump repeatedly stated that he favored immigration: *"but they have to come legally"*, making it clear that he opposed only *illegal* immigration. But the media continued falsely to denounce him as *'anti-immigrant'*.

BUILDING A WALL
Trump was also attacked, and denounced as 'divisive', for proposing to build a wall on the U.S. southern border to prevent illegal immigrants from entering the U.S. through its southern border with Mexico.

"We need to build bridges, not walls," Hillary Clinton declaimed, and repeated it at practically every rally she held.

She knew, and the news media new, that she was deceiving the American people, because she knew, and the news media knew, that Congress enacted the *Secure Fence Act of 2006*, and a separate homeland security spending bill to pay for the fence, pursuant to which about 650 miles of fencing *was built* on the U.S. border with Mexico.[134] Hillary Clinton and the news media also knew, but concealed from the public that Hillary Clinton had voted for the bill that was enacted into law as the *Secure Fence Act of 2006*.[135] Does anyone imagine that Andrea Mitchell or Chuck Todd or Jake Tapper or Wolf Blitzer or Chris Mathews or Rachel Maddow didn't know these facts? But on and on they went demonizing Trump for proposing to build a wall in America's southern border with Mexico.

---

134 http://www.politifact.com/truth-o-meter/statements/2011/may/16/barack-obama/obama-says-border-fence-now-basically-complete/
135 https://www.wsws.org/en/articles/2006/10/wall-o04.html

Now, it is true that the fence didn't work, and didn't stop anyone from coming illegally into the U.S. But Congress's intention was not to enact a token fence, a pretend barrier to immigration: Congress enacted the *Secure Fence Act of* 2006 and legislation to pay for it to stop illegal immigration. All Trump was proposing was to do what others had already proposed to do except do it properly—rather like with the Wollman ice rink in New York City's Central Park.

The site of what became the Wollman ice rink was used for outdoor summer events until it was closed in 1980 for renovations that were projected to take two years and cost $9.1 million. Six years later, after spending $13 million on the project, the city still hadn't completed the job, and that's when Trump stepped in, and completed it in six months—ahead of schedule and under budget—spending $2.25 million instead of the projected $2.5 million of his own money. New York City, like Congress, wasn't intentionally being incompetent, and Trump was only doing effectively what the New York City tried but couldn't do at all.

The wall Trump was proposing to build on the southern border was no different from the Wollman ice rink he built: those mocking him for it, saying it cannot be done, are the ones who voted for the useless fence on the U.S. southern border, and they are no different from the incompetent politicians who tried to build the Wollman ice rink in Central Park. When former New York City Mayor, Mike Bloomberg, the once Democrat turned Republican now Independent, mocked Trump saying he was a New Yorker and knew a con when he saw one, he had forgotten about the Wollman ice rink, and thinking like the politician looking for job.

Trump repeatedly said that he employed many Mexicans and loved the Mexican people because they were hard-working and devoted to their families. And Trump also repeatedly said that the Wall would have a big door in the middle so people can come in, "*but they have to come LEGALLY*".

In front of 24 million people, Trump said at the First Republican Debate hosted by Fox News,

> "*There will be a big, fat, beautiful door right in the middle of the Wall.*"

And he repeated it at the Third Republican Debate in Colorado, so the news media was in no doubt about that Trump was talking only about *illegal* immigrants, not *all* immigrants.[136]

Deporting Illegal Immigrants

Since coming to office in 2009, Obama's government has deported more than 2.5 million people, and is on pace to deport more people than the 19 presidents who governed the United States from 1892-2000 combined.[137] Two classes of illegal immigrants presented thorny problems that Obama sought to resolve with an executive order rather than work with Congress to pass comprehensive immigration reform as he had promised to do. In November, 2014, Obama issued an executive order to *prevent* the 'undocumented parents' of American citizens and permanent residents—i.e. those who entered the country illegally but whose children became citizens or permanent residents.[138]

---

136 http://time.com/4092571/republican-debate-immigration/

137 http://fusion.net/story/252637/obama-has-deported-more-immigrants-than-any-other-president-now-hes-running-up-the-score/

138 http://www.npr.org/sections/thetwo-way/2014/11/20/365519963/obama-will-announce-relief-for-up-to-5-million-immigrants

Eighteen months later, the courts struck down his executive order as exceeding the scope of presidential authority.[139]

So, Trump was hardly alone in believing that those who are in this country illegally should be deported. But, unlike others who believe that illegal immigrants should be required to leave, Trump repeatedly said that this should be done "humanely". He also proposed, in sharp contrast to some of his opponents like Texas Senator Ted Cruz, that illegal immigrants who haven't committed any crimes could come back, perhaps on an expedited basis, but they must come back legally.

Yet, the news media consistently tried to portray Trump as wanting to "round up" illegal immigrants, and referred to Trump proposal as entailing a special immigration force going around the country 'dragging people out of their homes'. But the news media, not Trump used these words and created these images, and it didn't fool members of the public that didn't share the news media's ideology.

It has been repeatedly pointed out that the social role of the news media is not only to provide citizens with the information they need to make decisions in their lives and govern themselves, but to build a community and create a forum for public criticism and compromise, but one that is also about solving the problems that people face in their daily lives.[140] By demonizing Trump and distorting his proposals, the news media actively prevented discussion of how solutions to a difficult social problem could be implemented.

---

139 http://www.nytimes.com/2016/06/24/us/supreme-court-immigration-obama-dapa.html?_r=0
140 Kovach & Rosenstiel, supra note 9 at 15-17 (page 13)

It is not hard to think of ways to deport illegal immigrants humanely, and link deportations to expedited means of reentry for those who have been law abiding and have children who were born or raised in this country—the so called 'dreamers'.

The process would begin with a notice to leave within a given time period— not 'rounding up' or 'dragging people out of their homes'. Incentives to leave voluntarily can easily be created by allowing those who pass background checks to return more quickly and to face a reduced fine. Leaving within a specified time period, and placing the names of those who leave voluntarily within that time period onto an immigration petition list in the order in which they left, would create further incentives for illegal immigrants to leave voluntarily and quickly, so the solution to the problem would be not dragged out for years as Trump demonizers have posited.

By demonizing and imputing evil motives to those who see things differently from them, the news media has helped turn a soluble logistical problem into an insoluble moral dilemma, and continues to erects serious social barrier to solving our social problems. The wider public is slowly beginning to get that.

MUSLIMG CELEBRATING ON 9/11

Trump made the statement about Muslims in New Jersey celebrating on 9/11 after the terrorist attack on Paris. The point of the remark wasn't to attack a religion: it was to emphasize that "*something is going on*" in the Muslim community, and we had to find out what it was.

Why? Because no normal person would celebrate an event that caused such destruction and so many people to lose their lives—no matter where the event occurred and no matter what the person's political views. That anyone would celebrate such an incident was symptomatic that something serious and perverse was going on—that was clearly the point Trump was trying to make.

Trump obviously exaggerated to make his point by referring to "thousands and thousands" of people celebrating, but that was a metaphor, a rhetorical flourish to make his point. It was not a statement meant to be taken literally because the *point* he was making was not *how many* people were celebrating the fall of the Twin Towers but that *anyone* would celebrate event like that at all was symptomatic of something—and we had to find out what it was.

If Trump had said "a number of people" were celebrating it may have been factually more accurate, but it would not have made the *point* he was trying to make as well. Trump stood by his story that he saw people celebrate the fall of the Twin Towers, but he never again claimed he saw "*thousands*" of Muslims celebrate after the rally, as he had made his point.

The news media spared nothing in denouncing Trump. There was *no evidence* that *anyone* had celebrated the fall of the Twin Towers on 9/11 in the U.S.: the news media asserted that as a fact categorically, emphatically, and repeatedly. The *Washington Post* took the lead in denouncing Trump as a liar, and wrote:

> "*But an extensive examination of news clips from that period **turns up NOTHING**. There were some reports of celebrations overseas, in Muslim countries, but **NOTHING that we can find***

involving the Arab populations of New Jersey except for un-confirmed reports."[141] (Boldface and capitalization added)

There was, in fact, quite extensive evidence available to the *Washington Post* from a number of sources that a number of people did celebrate the fall of the Twin Towers on 9/11 in New Jersey, confirming what Trump had said.

Mark Mueller, of *NJ Advanced Media*, interviewed more than two dozen people after Trump made his statement about seeing Muslims celebrate on 9/11. Mueller determined that although thousands of people clearly didn't celebrate, many did. The following were some of his findings:

1. A retired police captain, Peter Gallagher, said he cleared a rooftop celebration of 20 to 30 people at 6 Tonnele Avenue, a four-story apartment building with an unobstructed view of Lower Manhattan, in the hours after the second tower fell.

   "Some men were dancing, some held kids on their shoulders," Gallagher, who was a sergeant at the time, said. *"The women were shouting in Arabic and keening in the high-pitched wail of Arabic fashion. They were told to go back to their apartments since a crowd of non-Muslims was gathering on the sidewalk below and we feared for their safety."*

2. Ron Knight was one of two Tonnele Avenue residents who said they witnessed a crowd celebrating on John F. Kennedy Boulevard not far from Masjid Al-Salam, the mosque where

---

141 https://www.washingtonpost.com/news/fact-checker/wp/2015/11/22/donald-trumps-outrageous-claim-that-thousands-of-new-jersey-muslims-celebrated-the-911-attacks/

Omar Abdel-Rahman, known as the "blind sheikh," preached before the 1993 World Trade Center bombing.

3. Carlos Ferran, 60, a neighbor of Knight, was on his way to buy some beer when he saw the gathering on the sidewalk. *"Some of them had their hands in the air,"* Ferran said. *"They were happy."*

Paolo Guzmán, of WCBS in New York, aired a report in 2001 in which he said that an investigator had told him suspects were found on the roof of a Jersey City building with *"a model of the [World] Trade Center...They knew that the planes were going to hit, and they wanted a ring-side seat."*

"Just a couple of blocks away from that Jersey City apartment the F.B.I. raided yesterday and had evidence removed, there is another apartment building, one that investigators told me, quote, 'was swarming with suspects' — suspects who I'm told were cheering on the roof when they saw the planes slam into the Trade Center. Police were called to the building by neighbors and found eight men celebrating, six of them tenants in the building," Guzman reported in 2001.

"The F.B.I. and other terrorist task force agencies arrived, and the older investigators on the task force recalled that they had been to this building before, eight years ago, when the first World Trade Center attack led them to Sheik Omar Abdel-Rahman, whose Jersey City mosque lies between the two buildings getting attention today. And the older investigators remember that the suspects that eventually got convicted for the first Trade Center case ... lived in the building where these same eight men were celebrating the destruction that they saw from the roof. Calling this a hot address, the task force investigators ordered everyone detained."

Fifteen years later, in response to questions after Trump made his claims about Muslim celebrations on 9/11, Guzman attempted to 'walk back' his comments, claiming that he was just reporting rumors. However, Guzman tacitly acknowledged that the events he reported in 2001 did occur, only he was now discounting them:

> *"There were people in the New Jersey Muslim community who were happy the attacks happened,"* Guzman told Newsmax, and confirmed that he had interviewed them, but opined that *"they were outcasts from the greater Muslim population".*[142]

On October 28, 2001, the *New York Times* reported

> *"Within hours of the terror attacks, F.B.I. agents hurriedly intercepted telephone calls in which suspected associates of Al Qaeda **in the United States were overheard celebrating the attacks**. In the following days, agents swept in and arrested them."*[143] (Boldface added)

Rudy Giuliani and Bernie Kerik, who was New York Police Chief on 9/11, both confirmed that there were reports of celebrations in Brooklyn, Queens, as well as in Paterson, New Jersey.

Clearly, people in New Jersey did celebrate on 9/11, and the news media's claim to the contrary is false. Thousands of people may not have celebrated, but that does not make the *gist* of what Trump said false: some people were celebrating an event no reasonable person would celebrate, indicating that something was going on.

---

142 http://www.newsmax.com/Newsfront/trump-adviser-dan-scavino-proof/2015/12/02/id/704271/

143 New York Times, October 28, 2001, Section 1B; Column 1; Metropolitan Desk; Pg. 2.

THE MUSLIM BAN

The most strident denunciation of Trump came after his proposed 'Muslim Ban'. Trump made it perfectly clear that he always intended his Muslim ban to be *temporary*, and that his proposal was a safety measure intended to protect the public, and not an attack on religion or on Muslims. But to the news media, what *it* thought of the proposal, not the proposal that Trump actually made, became fact. The news media also repeatedly asserted as a *fact* that Trump's proposed ban was an unconstitutional attack on religion and all Muslims, and it was un-American. It was none of these things.

The day after Trump's speech, Eric Posner, a constitutional scholar and law professor at the Chicago Law School, addressed the question of the proposed ban's constitutionality, and concluded that the ban was probably *not* unconstitutional, contrary to what the news media was telling the public through is 'legal consultants'.

"The Supreme Court has held consistently, for more than a century, that constitutional protections that normally benefit Americans and people on American territory do not apply when Congress decides who to admit and who to exclude as immigrants or other entrants," Professor Posner wrote.[144]

"The Court has repeatedly turned away challenges to immigration statutes and executive actions on grounds that they discriminate on the basis of race, national origin, and political belief, and that they deprive foreign nationals of due process protections. While the Court has not ruled on religious discrimination, it has also never

---

144 http://ericposner.com/is-an-immigration-ban-on-muslims-unconstitutional/

given the slightest indication that religion would be exempt from the general rule."[145]

The news media's legal analysts, like MSNBC's Ari Melber, ignored the article, and continued to denounce Trump's proposal as unconstitutional in the most strident terms, conveying the impression to the public that this was a *fact*. Lamenting these assertions about the proposal's supposed unconstitutionality, Professor Posner wrote:

"Unfortunately, that is not what scholars—who certainly know better—are telling journalists. They are likely being abetted by journalists and headline writers who don't like the idea that Trump's ban would be lawful."[146]

But that is not all that Professor Posner wrote. He also pointed out that, far from being *un-American*, as Tom Brokaw and others in the news media repeatedly asserted with righteous indignation.

"There is even precedent for Trump's plan," Professor Posner wrote.

"In 1891, Congress passed a statute that made inadmissible people who practiced polygamy (directed, at the time, at Mormons), and in 1907 extended this ban to people "who admit their belief in the practice of polygamy. While Congress later repealed the latter provision (the former seems to be still on the books), no court—as far I know—ruled it unconstitutional."[147]

---

145 http://ericposner.com/is-an-immigration-ban-on-muslims-unconstitutional/
146 Id.
147 Id.

Writing in the *Washington Post*, Eugene Volokh added that the Court had also held it constitutional to exclude people based on their political beliefs.[148]

Hillary Clinton attempted to tap into the mass hysteria the news media was trying to incite about Trump's proposed Muslim ban and claimed that ISIS was using videos of Trump's proposal to help recruit followers. Like so much of her public statements, what Clinton told the public was a bald-faced lie, and the news media did slightly rap Clinton on the knuckles for that fabrication. But, although there was no evidence that ISIS was using Trump's proposed Muslim ban in propaganda videos to attract followers, there *was*, ironically, evidence that Hillary Clinton's husband, Bill Clinton—and George W. Bush—were pictured in Islamic terrorist propaganda videos, but only Fox News aired the videos: MSNBC and CNN did not even mention them. Evidently, it was not the kind of information they wanted to report about a candidate they were actively supporting.

ALLEGATIONS OF RACISM

Trump has been in the public eye for over 30 years, and had never been accused of being a racist before his presidential bid. Bill O'Reilly, Geraldo Rivera, Larry King and others in the Media who know Trump have said in public that they have never known Trump say or do anything to suggest that he was a racist. Nor had anyone ever accused Trump of being a racist before Jake Tapper tried to make him out to be a racist just before the Super Tuesday primaries. But Tapper knew that Trump wasn't a racist. There was

---

148 https://www.washingtonpost.com/news/volokh-conspiracy/wp/2015/12/08/banning-muslims-from-entering-the-u-s-is-a-very-bad-idea-but-it-may-be-constitutionally-permissible/

ample evidence in the public domain proving that Trump wasn't and never had been a racist, and Tapper was well aware of that evidence.

For example, in 2000, Donald Trump was interviewed by the *New York Times* about why he didn't join the Reform Party and run for President. Trump replied:

> *"So the Reform Party now includes a Klansman, Mr. Duke, a neo-Nazi, Mr. Buchanan, and a communist, Ms. Fulani. This is not company I wish to keep."*

In a separate interview with Matt Lauer, Trump said this about David Duke and the Reform Party:

> *"Well, you've got David Duke just joined—a bigot, a racist, a problem. I mean, this is not exactly the people you want in your party."*

Fast forward to August 26, 2015, when NBC news reported that David Duke had said on his radio program that Trump was *"the best of the lot"*. Trump was questioned about Duke's statement by Bloomberg news:

> *"I don't need his endorsement, I certainly wouldn't want his endorsement,"* Trump said.[149]

Trump was next confronted with the fact that white supremacist groups were enthusiastic about his candidacy, and pressed on whether

---

149 http://www.politico.com/story/2015/08/donald-trump-doesnt-want-david-duke-endorsement-121784

he thought there was something about his message was resonating with those groups. Trump replied,

"I hope there's not."

So Tapper knew that Trump wasn't a racist, even if the *New York Times* and *Washington Post* were trying to make him out to be one because some White Supremacists groups had said some positive things about his candidacy. Tapper never asked Trump outright if he would denounce the KKK, and then accused Trump of racism for ostensibly failing to denounce the KKK.

In a later interview, when Wolf Blitzer confronted Trump with his ostensible failure to denounce white supremacy groups, Trump exposed the attacks of racism for the contrivances they were:

Blitzer: *"Why do you think these various white-supremacist groups are supporting your campaign?"*

Trump: *"I mean, you're telling me this, but I don't know why. I'm the least racist person you'll ever meet."*

Blitzer: *"You condemn them? You don't want their support?"*

Trump: *"Of course I condemn them. Always, I've always condemned them. I don't want their support, I don't need their support."*[150]

Two months after this interview with Wolf Blitzer, the *Washington Post* published what it called an 'audit' of Trump's statements about white

---

150 http://www.businessinsider.com/wolf-blitzer-donald-trump-donald-trump-cnn-interview-2016-3

supremacists in interviews over the years, but the Post assiduously omitted mention or reference to this interview with Wolf Blitzer.[151] And despite this record of never having anything to do with and denouncing racists groups, Jake Tapper persisted with his accusations of racism against Trump based on Trump's belief that a judge of Mexican heritage, who had publically expressed pride in his national heritage and was a member of an interest group advocating for illegal immigrants, *La Raza lawyers of California*. The bogusness of Tapper's position was exposed by Supreme Court Justice Sonia Sotomayor's stated belief that her "Latina" heritage would likely affect the facts she saw and her judging.

Trump had given countless numbers of interviews from which the public could judge for itself whether or not he was a racist. It was perfectly obvious that Trump wasn't, and the news media's attempt to portray Trump a racist likely back fired at a time when President Obama was dividing the country along racial lines, and race relations had deteriorated to a point not seen since the 1960s.

INCITING VIOLENCE

Shortly after its unsuccessful attempt to make Trump out to be a racist, the news media tried falsely to portray Trump as inciting violence at his rallies. It was a short-lived, disingenuous attempt made by misrepresentations of events, and an abject failure of the news media to investigate violent incidents to find out which specific groups were responsible for them.

The news media failed to investigate who was responsible when violence first reared its ugly head at the rally Trump had planned to

---

151 https://www.washingtonpost.com/news/fact-checker/wp/2016/03/01/donald-trump-and-david-duke-for-the-record/

hold in Chicago. Who were they? Hillary supporters? Bernie supporters? Members or Moveon.org or Black Lives Matter? The news media did nothing to find that out. Like everyone else, the news media had a good idea who the rioters were but didn't want to find out for sure because they were groups ideologically in tune with the news media whose violence the news media has never unequivocally condemned.

Then, the news media seized on the first and only actual violent act by a Trump supporter, and distorted what happened by taking part of a comment Trump had made a month earlier and making it appear that he had said it in a very different context, and caused the Trump supporter to punch a protester who had given him the middle finger, as described in Chapter 20.

The news media exploited the mayhem that Bernie supporters, Black Lives Matter advocates, and paid rioters were trying to cause at Trump rallies in Arizona and California, until Trump supporters were so savagely attacked at a rally in San Diego that not even the news media could turn facts on their head and make such obvious victims of violence out to be its perpetrators.

Trump had secured the nomination by then, but what was so obvious in San Diego had been obvious to most people in Chicago and Arizona and earlier rallies in California—that Trump supporters do not try to stop other candidates from speaking by going to their rallies and shouting them down; and Trump supporters didn't attack the police and cause property damage. They were caused by those advocating ideas and supporting candidates the news media endorses.

News Media Myths

"The fancy cannot cheat so well as she is famed to do," wrote Keats in *Ode to a Nightingale*. It explains why the many myths created by the news media about Trump were so ineffective in derailing his candidacy. Numerous negative stories about Trump were about statements he never made: they were the news media's interpretations of what he said that did not give his statements their plain meaning, as, for example, with Trump's use of the word "*schlonged*". Many of them probably struck the public as absurd, like the assertion by about Trump's reference to Megyn Kelly's periods.

The absurdity of this interpretation is particularly transparent as there is a legal rule for interpreting general terms like 'wherever' that the news media interpreted as referring to menstruation. The rule has a fancy Latin name—*ejusdem generis noscitur a sociis*—which stands for the principle that the meaning of words is determined from the company they keep, and where a general word is linked to specific one, then it should be interpreted to mean the same sort of thing as the specific word.

Trump used the expression "blood coming out of her eyes" as a metaphor for Kelly's hostility towards him, and added 'or wherever', and what goes with 'eyes' is 'ears' or 'nose', not uterus. So a court, for example, would never have interpreted 'wherever' in the perverted way the news media and Romney interpreted it. Kelly, a lawyer, of course, knew this.

The relentlessness and sheer excess of the news media's onslaught on Trump, twisting and distorting every word he said whenever possible to reflect negatively on him—so evident in NBC's millennial journalists' endless tweets about Trump— slowly but inexorably eroded the credibility of the media and turned much of the public against it. Repeating weak arguments make them less, not more persuasive; and you also can't fool all the people all the time. By dribs and drabs, the falsity and distortions of what was said about Trump became manifest over time to those with no axe to grind.

CHAPTER 35

Why the Political Class Failed: A Question of Leadership

• • •

There are two kinds of leaders: those who are interested in the flock, and those who are interested in the fleece.

ANON

WHY COULDN'T THE REPUBLICAN ESTABLISHMENT, the Never Trump activists, and their SuperPacs stop Trump? Why couldn't sixty-four thousand negative advertisements, almost daily character attacks on Trump by prominent Republicans, the declared intent by senior members of the Bush administrations to vote for Hillary Clinton instead of Trump, and declamations by prominent Conservatives that they would leave the party if Trump was nominated, bring down a novice with no political experience?

What on earth was going on? Was it because, as former Florida Congressman Joe Scarborough put it, Trump's opponents were *"a bunch of goofballs, who don't talk straight to the American people, who can only say what they've memorized or focus groups told them to say"?*

No one in the news media really knew, and they had certainly never seen or heard of anything like what was happening in the primaries before. But that did not deter them from flooding the airwaves with simplistic—'tapping into'—theories to explain Trump's appeal as soon as the news media stopped treating his candidacy as entertainment and dismissing it as a 'joke'.

People still hurting from the Great Recession were angry—so Trump was tapping into their anger. People didn't trust Washington politicians—so Trump was tapping into anti-Washington sentiment. People were concerned about growing racial tensions in the country—so Trump was tapping into racial fears. People were concerned about their future and turning on immigrants—so Trump was tapping into anti-immigrant feelings.

These trite explanations were repeated, day after day, on the cable news networks by the same political operatives —Anna Navarro, S.E. Cupp, Erick Erickson, Anthony van Jones, Karen Finney, Hillary Rosen, Paul Begala, Donna Brazile, and others—and the same opinion writers—George Will, Charles Krauthammer, Dana Milbank, Thomas Friedman, Nicholas Kristoff, and others. Some, like the *New York Times* writer, David Brooks, who has made a career explaining other people's theories of social phenomena to lay audiences, offered a more highfalutin analysis of Trump's psychology or personality:

"It's hard to know exactly what is going on in that brain, but science lends a clue," he opined grandiloquently. *"Psychologists wonder*

if narcissists are defined by extremely high self-esteem or by extremely low self-esteem that they are trying to mask. The current consensus seems to be that they are marked by unstable self-esteem. Their self-confidence can be both high and fragile, so they perceive ego threat all around.".[152]

This is where Elizabeth Warren seems to have got her idea to denounce Trump as an *"insecure little man"*—she obviously didn't realize that she was repeating nonsensical psychobabble and that Duke University's Professor Allen Frances had called on Brooks to *"stop being an amateur psychologist"*.

"What Brooks doesn't know about psychology is a lot. Everything he says about it has a shallow ring, is misinformed, and displays the same bias and ulterior motive,"[153] Frances wrote.

Michael Barone, the conservative analyst who wrote *The Almanac of American Politics*, had a more sophisticated theory to "make sense of the electoral divisions" which, he noted, "don't fall on traditional lines".[154] He posited that Trump appealed to people who were less socially connected, meaning that he appealed to groups that had low social capital.

Barone based his conclusion on Trump's poor showing in 13 states highest in social capital like the Dutch-American counties in northwest and central Iowa, and strong showing in 11 states with low social connectedness (except Cruz's home state of Texas). However, Barone noted that all but one (West Virginia) of the low social

---

152 http://wex.theoklahomapubli.netdna-cdn.com/david-brooks-calls-trump-a-narcissist-assesses-candidates-mental-stability/article/2596931
153 Id.
154 http://www.nationalreview.com/article/433334/donald-trumps-appeal-lower-among-socially-connected

connectedness states had voted, and that 7 of the 13 high social connectedness states had yet to vote. Unfortunately for Barone's theory, Trump won all those high social connectedness states, and, like all the other post-hoc explanations for statistical findings, it didn't stand the test of time.

The news media 'experts' supported their 'tapping-into' theories by telling television audiences that the typical Trump supporter was a poorly educated, blue-collar white male earning a below average wage, who felt disenfranchised and angry. They were part of the social group who saw their life expectancy fall in recent years, not from 'big killers' like diabetes and heart disease, but from suicides and the ravages of drug addiction, alcoholism and liver disease[155]— the culmination of the declining fortunes of poorly educated white American males.[156]

The news media sold this stereotype to the public by preferentially singling out unkempt, white males covered in tattoos from the thousands who regularly attended Trump's rallies, and the stereotype quickly became an accepted 'fact'. But the news media's stereotype was based on a fallacy— the *'base rate fallacy'*: a technical term for a very simple concept.[157]

Only 30% of the general population is college educated.[158] This educational *'base rate'* affects the proportion of college-educated

---

155 http://www.nytimes.com/2015/11/03/health/death-rates-rising-for-middle-aged-white-americans-study-finds.html

156 http://www.nytimes.com/2012/09/21/us/life-expectancy-for-less-educated-whites-in-us-is-shrinking.html

157 See e.g. Daniel Kahneman, Thinking Fast and Slow, Farrar, Strauss & Giroux New York, 2011.

158 http://www.politifact.com/truth-o-meter/statements/2015/apr/08/rick-santorum/70-americans-dont-have-college-degree-rick-santoru/

and college non-educated individuals in any sample of voters, as the following example illustrates.

If, for example, 50% of non-college educated voters, and 80% of college-educated voters vote for a candidate in an area, and 10,000 people in that area vote, the candidate would get 3500 non-college educated (50% of 7000), and 2400 college-educated votes (80% of 3000)— assuming that 30% of the inhabitants in that area were college educates as in the general population. So, even though 30% more college-educated than non-college educated voters voted for that candidate, a higher proportion of that candidate's voters would still be non-college educated (3500/5900 = 59%) than college educated (2400/5900=41%) —all because of the *'base' rate'* of college-educated individuals in the area. The news media simply didn't seem to understand this or want to understand it.

News media experts explained how this minority of disenfranchised voters—the stereotypical Trump supporter— was able to propel Trump into the lead in the polls on a '3 lane theory'. According to this theory, there was a crowded 'Establishment lane' of governors and senators, and they (Jeb Bush, Marco Rubio, and others) were dividing the traditional Republican vote. The 'non-Establishment lane' was divided into a Trump lane and the non-Trump lane comprised of Dr. Ben Carson, Senator Ted Cruz, and, to a lesser extent, Carly Fiorina. But, the aggregate non-Establishment vote was over 50%, which indicated to the news media pundits that the electorate was fed up with conventional politics and the gridlock in Washington, and was confirmed by Congress's 9% approval rate in the polls. Everyone bought into this '3 lane theory', and when Scott Walker dropped out of the race in September, 2015, he implored his party to coalesce and unite behind one candidate.

As late as December, 2015, Karl Rove, the 'wunderkind' credited with George W. Bush's electoral success and a Trump opponent, was telling television viewers that the maximum proportion of primary Republican votes Trump could get had about a 30% 'ceiling'. Rove used simple calculations on a hand-held white board to 'prove' this, and beguile his audience into believing that his predictions were 'scientific' and not merely educated guesses—(and convinced himself too, to judge by how Rove confronted Fox News's statisticians on live television during the 2012 election, insisting that they were wrong in predicting victory for Obama). But Rove was wrong again. He no more understood why Trump was leading in the polls than any of the other news media 'experts'.

Politico seems to have been the first to question the Trump-supporter stereotype on March 3, 2016, based on the exit polling that became available after the Super Tuesday primaries.[159] *Politico* pointed out that in these polls Trump was the most popular candidate among college-educated voters in six states, and second in another six.

"A large number of college Republicans count themselves as Trump supporters," Politico wrote. But the authors, obviously ignorant of the 'base rate fallacy', added

"Still, voters without a college education are Trump's core base of support. **More non-college-educated voters than ones with college degrees have supported Trump in every single primary and caucus so far, according to exit polls.**"[160] (Boldface added)

---

159 http://www.politico.com/story/2016/03/5-myths-about-trump-supporters-220158
160 Id., supra note 159.

Of course—because there were more non-college educated than college educated voters among the people who voted.

Two months later, the statistician Nate Silver presented a more comprehensive refutation of the Trump-supporter stereotype based on exit polling from 23 primary states.[161] These exit polls found that:

1. The median household income of Trump supporters, $72,000, is well above the national median household income of about $56,000;
2. In each state, the median income of Trump supporters exceeded the median income for the state;
3. Forty-four percent of Trump supporters had college degrees, higher than the 33% of non-Hispanic white adults, or 29% of American adults overall, who have at least a bachelor's degree.

Still, NBC attempted to keep the Trump supporter myth alive by trying to reconcile the stereotype with exit polling data. NBC's theory was based on the unverified claim that the people who backed Trump early were *"very different from the united GPO block he now commands"*.[162]

This claim, and its statistical significance, are impossible to verify from the information NBC provided to the public, but it was based on arbitrarily dividing the states that voted between February 1 and May 3, 2016 into two groups—those voting between February 1st and March 15th, and those voting between March 15th and May 3rd—and imputing causal significance to the differences observed

---

161 The states were: NH, SC, AL, AR, CT, FL, GA, IL, MA, MI, MO, MS, NC, NY, OH, OK, PA, SC, TX, TN, VA, VT, WI. Data were also available for two caucus states, IA & NV, but they were less extensive, and Silver excluded them.

162 http://www.nbcnews.com/specials/donald-trump-republican-party

between these arbitrarily created groups. But anyone who has taken 101 statistics in college should know that correlation does not mean causation, and that the methodology NBC used, and the inference it drew from its findings are invalid.

Nevertheless, NBC tried vigorously to sell the theory on social media that

> *"The story of Trump is about a committed minority of Republican voters, whose existence was routinely ignored, gradually taking over the entire party."*[163]

To NBC's reporters—Benjy Sarlin, Katy Tur, Ari Melber, Kristen Welker—and others, this theory explained the Trump phenomenon: the Republican Establishment realized too late what was happening, and acted too late to try to stop Trump—too late because by the time it realized what was happening these blue collar, college-uneducated, angry white Trump-supporter had taken over the Republican Party. There was no need to look for deeper explanations: it was as simple as that—and it was nonsense.

Angry people—college-educated or not— who are only against something, and not 'for' anything, do not stand peacefully in line for eight to ten hours in the freezing cold or sweltering heat to hear a political candidate speak, as Trump supporters did in their thou- sands, rally after rally throughout the primaries, and in ever growing numbers. Angry people who are only against something do what the Black Lives Matter, Moveon.org, and other left wing activists did in Chicago and California, and tried to do in Arizona—attack Trump supporters and the police, smash and destroy property, set cars on

---

163 Id.

fire, riot, cause mayhem, and burn everything to the ground. Trump supporters never did that: they were the victims of violence, not its perpetrators—with the exception of one old man who'd had enough of being mocked and demonized, and 'sucker punched' a protester who had given him the middle finger.

The peculiarities of the 2015-16 primary political season—why Trump and Bernie Sanders attracted huge crowds to their rallies; why so many well-qualified candidates never polled above 1%-2%; why the Republican candidate with the best resume of then all, John Kasich, never gained any traction; and why Ted Cruz, despite having the best organization anyone had ever seen, never made it to the finish line despite his herculean, and often successful, attempts to manipulate the system to his advantage and defy how the electorate had voted—are best explained by the concepts about leadership developed by the political scientist and leadership scholar, James MacGregor Burns, in his Pulitzer Prize winning book, *Leadership*,[164] and other seminal works. [165]

Burns distinguished between exercises of power—which power seekers do to promote their interests and not the interests of their followers—and two types of leadership: *'transactional'* and *'transformational'*.[166]

Transactional leaders essentially act as brokers, and view their relationship with followers as an exchange relationship in which they offer followers what they value in exchange for their votes. What defines the relationship is not what is offered in exchange for

---

164 James MacGregor Burns, Leadership, Harper Row Publishers, N.Y. 1978.
165 James MacGregor Burns, Transforming Leadership, Grove Press, N.Y. 2003.
166 Id. at 22-27

votes—whether this is economic (like higher minimum wage), social (like maternity leave) or psychological (like LGBTQ rights)—but that the relationship is one of exchange. This is the most common type of leadership, and in business is called management. It was the kind of leadership the country was willing to settle for in 2008 when it elected Barak Obama.

Back in 2008, the country was exhausted by eight years of futile wars that had no end in sight, and that were draining the country's human and material resources. The country, desperate for a new direction, bought into Barack Obama's message of Hope and Change, and elected him the first African-American President of the United States. And they elected not just any black president: they elected an African-American who had been steeped in radical thought during his formative years, whose pastor's sermons were filled with anti-American hate speech—and they elected him not once but twice, hoping to move the country beyond racial divisions into a united post-racial world. But it didn't work out that way.

It didn't take the country long to realize that it had elected a person with oratorical not leadership or even managerial skills. The quality of leadership is measured by how much promised change is actually accomplished, and by that measure Obama had failed as a leader—even his one significant legislative accomplishment, *'Obamacare'*, was failing to deliver what it had promised.

During the first two years of his Presidency, when both the House and Senate were Democrat, Obama could have passed immigration reform, which he had promised to do, but chose healthcare reform instead, and signed into law *Obamacare*, which had passed Congress without a single Republican vote. The launch of *Obamacare* proved to be a 5 billion dollar disaster, and led to the resignation of Kathleen Sebelius, Obama's Health and Human Services Secretary. Like the VA hospital scandals that were to follow, it called into question Obama's managerial as well as his leadership skills.

However much ideological or partisan some of the opposition to *Obamacare* may have been, it was becoming indisputable that the simplistic premise on which it was based did not work out as its proponents had promised, and the representations Obama had made to the public about '*Obamacare*'—that those who already had health insurance would not be affected, and could keep their insurance and doctors—turned out not to be true.

About two years after *Obamacare* was enacted, it started to become clear that increased health care coverage had not led to greater access to health care, which was the whole point of *Obamacare*, because the low-cost insurance packages low income people could afford had such high deductibles that they could not afford to pay the deductibles and use their health plans.[167] The theory underlying the program—that forcing people to obtain health insurance or face a financial penalty would pay for program —also didn't work as Obama promised it would. Large health insurer left the market,[168] causing some people to lose their health insurance or doctors, and others saw their health insurance premiums double or triple. In short, *Obamacare*, President Obama's signature legislation was not producing the results promised, and was in serious trouble.

---

167 http://dailysignal.com/2014/12/09/proof-obamacare-increasing-coverage-not-access-health-care/
168 http://www.politico.com/story/2016/04/unitedhealth-drops-most-obamacare-business-222130

Not surprisingly, Obama got, in his own words, "schalacked" in the 2010 midterm elections. Obama lost the House of Representatives to the Republicans, and narrowly held on to the Senate with a majority of one, but caused the Tea Party to come into being. Two years later, Obama won re-election against Mitt Romney, a weak, uninspiring candidate who stood for nothing, but he lost the Senate to the Republicans.

Complete gridlock in Washington followed: Congress couldn't pass any legislation and nothing got done. Despite the ending of the wars in Afghanistan and Iraq, and the cut backs in military spending, the national debt doubled after Obama took office. Terrorism was growing around the world, and people didn't feel safe. Police were being assassinated in the streets of American cities, and race relations in the U.S. were the worst they had ever been since the 1960s — much of it caused by President Obama's misguided rhetoric.

The country was in serious trouble again, and polls were showing that 70%-80% of the public thought the country was on the wrong track[169]— but President Obama didn't see it that way. He told the country that people were living at a time in history when they were safer, healthier and better educated than ever before. He and his wife mocked Trump's slogan, 'Make American Great Again', saying that America was already great and flourishing, with a growing economy and 15 million new jobs created since he came into office.

Two days after Obama painted this rosy picture of the economy at the Democrat National Convention in Philadelphia, it was announced that the Gross Domestic Product (GDP) had grown by only

---

169 http://www.nytimes.com/2016/07/30/upshot/how-unhappy-are-americans-and-what-does-it-mean-for-the-election.html

1.2% in the second quarter of 2016, half of what had been forecast, and that the GDP in the first quarter was revised down to 0.8%. The forecast for the year as a whole was 1%, the lowest growth in GDP since 1949.

The day after President Obama said that people today were historically safer than at any time before, his own Director of National Intelligence, retired General James Clapper, said he was *"concerned about stability in the U.S. and the fragility of American institutions,"* calling them *"under assault."*[170]

Clapper said that parameters used by the intelligence community were indicating that about two-thirds of the countries around the world exhibited some instability, and added,

> *"I guess if you apply that same measure against us, well, we are starting to exhibit some of them, too. We pride ourselves on the institutions that have evolved over hundreds of years and I do worry about the, you know, fragility of those institutions."*[171]

Americans were desperate for leadership—but not any kind of leadership this time: they wanted what Professor Burns called transformational leadership, and no one besides Trump and Bernie Sanders were offering this kind of leadership.

John Kasich made the clearest case for his candidacy, but gave people the same reason to vote for him as Hillary Clinton gave for voting for her—experience. Kasich said he knew how to fix the

---

170 http://www.cnn.com/2016/07/29/politics/james-clapper-intel-chief-worried-instability-us/
171 http://www.cnn.com/2016/07/29/politics/james-clapper-intel-chief-worried-instability-us/

country's problems because he had balanced budgets before, and had turned a deficit in Ohio into a surplus. Yet, although he stayed in to the bitter end, Kasich could not win a single state besides his own state of Ohio. Why?

Because what Kasich was offering was good management, transactional leadership: you vote for me, and I will give you good management. He had a much better claim on that than Hillary Clinton, but people were looking for a transformational leader, not a manager.

Managers apply standard operating procedures to solve previously encountered problems: what Keith Grint calls 'tame' problems.[172] These are like puzzles with known solutions. They may be complicated, but they always have individual solutions, and the job of managers is to provide a process by which to solve the problem. Congress was packed with managers who couldn't get anything done—because they were not facing 'tame' problems.

The country was facing what Grint calls 'wicked' problems— defined in part by the very absence of *known* solutions. These are intractable problems that involve a great deal of uncertainty, and no clear cause and effect relationships.[173] They have no stopping point at which one can say that the problem has been solved, making those, like Jeb Bush, who confidently declared "*I can fix Washington*" sound simplistic, if not ridiculous.

'Wicked' problems cut across different cultures and institutions, and can't be solved by people who are trapped by their cultural

---

172 http://leadershipforchange.org.uk/wp-content/uploads/Keith-Grint-Wicked-Problems-handout.pdf

173 Id.

preferences into how to solve problems. To solve wicked problems requires

"engaging a community to face up to a complex collective problem, and requires the construction of innovative responses to novel or recalcitrant problems."[174]

It requires, *"a creative leader-follower interaction in which the leader offers initiatives that are not ordinarily part of day-to-day discourse, and that followers pick up, amplify, reshape, and direct back onto the leader"*[175]— in other words, transformative leadership.

None of Trump's opponents were offering this kind of leadership. Lindsey Graham, the one with the clearest and simplest reason for running, was asking Americans to vote for him because he could defeat ISIS. He dressed the exchange he was offering voters in patriotic rhetoric, but couldn't hide that it was still just a deal: elect me and I will defeat ISIS. That was it—and that's why he never got more than 1% in any poll. Defeating ISIS was a 'wicked' problem.

Carly Fiorina had a flash in the pan performance during the First Republican 'undercard' debate, showing voters that she had a firm grasp of the issues, was articulate and a good debater, which propelled her transiently to as high as 7% in some polls. But, she couldn't make up her mind about what she was offering voters: was she running because she was a woman, because she understood modern technology and business, or because she understood and could reform the Washington bureaucracy? Whichever it was, she was,

---

174 http://leadershipforchange.org.uk/wp-content/uploads/Keith-Grint-Wicked-Problems-handout.pdf
175 Burns, supra note 165 at 116-169 (page 194)

like Kasich, offering transactional leadership, a deal—you vote for me, and I'll clean up the mess in Washington.

The other candidates used a variety of rhetorical devices to make the deal they were offering voters sound like innovative solutions to the wicked problems facing the country, but they didn't convince anyone, which is why none of them could garner more than a few percentage points in the polls, and not because there were so many of them running for president, as the pundits said.

Voters don't vote on the basis of policy proposals: they vote based on values. Trump and Bernie Sanders were the only candidates offering a value laden vision for the country, and that's why they were the only candidates who attracted tens of thousands of people to their rallies. Their visions were, to be sure, very different, but they were none the less transformative for that. They both inspired their followers to rise above narrow self-interest and work together for a transcending goal, but when the pundits saw their rallies, they saw only large crowds, not empowered followers, and didn't understand what was going on.

For Bernie Sanders that goal was to make society fairer and transform the U.S. into a democratic socialist country like many in Europe, in which higher education, like health care, was free, and in which the middle class had a larger share of the country's wealth than was presently going to the top 1% of the population.

For Trump, that goal was to Make America Great Again by making Americans winners again—winners in trade with China, Japan, and Mexico by renegotiating trade deals; winners on the world stage by building up the military, restructuring NATO to ensure that member countries pay their fair share and focus their attention on terrorism so ISIS is defeated; winners at home by rebuilding our roads, bridges, tunnels and airports, making health care more affordable, taking care of Veterans, and ensuring law and order.

People who attacked Trump's proposals by attacking him personally, claiming he did not represent American "values" confused private virtue with the public values politicians are concerned with. Virtue refers to norms of private conduct: chastity, sobriety, cleanliness, self-control, honesty in personal relationships; public values are order, liberty, equality, justice, pursuit of happiness.[176]

To attack Trump's vision for the country because of his past womanizing, for example, as the *New York Times* tried to do, is more a reflection on the vulgarity of our culture—especially of those in the news media—than on Trump. JFK was a notorious womanizer, and committed adultery as President: so was FDR, but their womanizing wasn't a topic of public discourse because our culture and press were less vulgar back then.

Policy proposals are not ends in themselves, but means to ends, and that's how voters judge them—in terms of what it tells them about the public values a candidate stands for. Trump's proposal to build a wall or prevent Muslims from entering the country, for example, were means to an end—maintaining the territorial integrity of the country, preventing illegal immigration, ensuring public safety and security. They were not ends in themselves—racial policies targeting ethnic groups because of their race or religion, as the news media tried to make them out to be. Most of the public got that.

---

176 Burns, supra note 165 at 28 (page 194)

The interaction between transforming leaders and their follow-ers is a powerful causal force for change. Transformational leaders take the initiative; they mobilize people for participation in the pro-cess of change by creating a sense of collective identity; they make their followers feel empowered by creating in them stronger feelings of self-worth and self-efficacy, making their lives and work seem more meaningful. Transformative leaders don't exercise power over their followers, but champion and inspire them to rise above narrow self-interest and work together for a transcending goal.[177] This is what Trump and Bernie did, and why the Republican Party and the news media couldn't stop Trump's nomination.

---

177 Burns, supra note 165 at 25-27 (page 194)

CHAPTER 36

Trump's Appeal: A Question of Identity

• • •

If you can dream— but not make dreams your master
If you can think—but not make thoughts your aim
If you can meet with Triumph and Disaster
And treat these two impostors just the same

RUDYARD KIPLING

THE NEWS MEDIA AND POLITICAL class were unable to stop Trump's nomination for another reason—the bond between Trump and his followers was unshakable. Yes, Trump said thing that made his most ardent followers cringe; he could be crude and crass and act as if his IQ had suddenly halved. But it didn't make the slightest bit of difference. His followers could no more abandon him than a mother could abandon a preschooler who'd said something really embarrassing, really loudly at the supermarket checkout counter. Why? Because the image Trump projected resonated with his supporters' self-image as Americans, and their image of America's national identity.

The political battle waged during this election was not over competing policy proposals, but over America's national identity. Hillary Clinton didn't respond to Trump's proposal to build a wall on the U.S. border with Mexico with her own proposals for immigration reform: she countered it with the slogan, *"we want to build bridges not walls"* to convey a different image from Trump of *'who we are"*.

There are many components to a person's identity or self-image, and one of them is national identity. Americans hold differing and competing beliefs about their national identity. In the past, they resolved these differences politically, and were able to hammer out a consensus over America's image because their loyalty to their country superseded their private interests and loyalty to ethnic groups,[178] and believed that what united them was greater than what divided them.

But no more. Disagreements over America's identity—who we are as a people, and what kind of society we want to create—have become so divergent in an age of political correctness, and discourse over it so 'uncivil', as to make the differences irreconcilable. Social scientists no longer find ideological overlap between the two political parties,[179] and 'incivility' is just a weak word to describe the instability of a society that cannot resolve competing images of its national identity through its existing political institutions.

Identity politics has become the norm. It originates in people's need to have their inner, 'authentic' selves publically recognized whenever they feel the norms of the surrounding society conflicting

---

178 Francis Fukuyama, Political Order and Political Decay, Farrar, Straus & Gioux, New York, 2014, p 186

179 http://www.pewresearch.org/fact-tank/2014/06/12/7-things-to-know-about-polarization-in-america/

with their 'true' inner selves.[180] People experiencing such conflicts demand public recognition of their identity and that it be given equal dignity and legal status, as happened most recently with the LGBTQ community.

This election cycle, Trump supporters are making the same kind of demand: for their identity to be given equal dignity and legal status, because they feel their interests and voice drowned by the din of identity politics and the clamoring of special interests. Who these Trump supporters are has been difficult to pin down because they are not part of an easy-to-identify group with a salient characteristic, like the LGBTQ community or ethnic minorities. They cut across familiar demographic and 'identity' groups: it is why evangelicals supported Trump, and Peter Thiel, the billionaire co-founder of PayPal, declared himself at the Republican National Convention proud to be gay, a Republican, and an American.

America's national identity was never founded on ethnicity as it was in Europe and South America, but on the great Enlightenment principles of equality, fairness, and justice. Trump supporters are united in rejecting the identity politics and image of their country being created by the news media and today's Democrat politicians. They feel marginalized and as aliens in their own country. They feel mocked and rejected for who they are by an entitled class trying paint them as un-American. Trump has been the catalyst that united them in a collective consciousness of who they were. That is why Trump supporters travel long distances to his rallies and queue quietly for long hours under inclement conditions to hear him speak—because Trump makes them feel empowered and not because they are 'angry'.

---

180 Fukuyama, supra note 177 at 186 (page 201).

Americans have always seen themselves as winners, and their country as the greatest the world has ever known: a country of inventors and entrepreneurs, where great fortunes can be built by those born into poverty; where anyone can be anything they want to be that their God-given talents and efforts allow them to be. That is the national image that Trump projects, and that is the image that resonates with his supporters.

Trump may not personally embody a collective national identity, but his message does—although quite a few of his traits do resonate with American's self-image—the fighter who never gives up; the tough guy with a soft heart; the blue collar billionaire who eats Kentucky Fried Chicken on his private jet, and knows how to drive a Caterpillar and lay sheetrock; the winner who can be vulgar and a buffoon, but who's really savvy and smart. There's something of John Wayne in him, and it's John Wayne, not David Niven that most Americans identify with.

But it is his defiant complaint that "We Don't Win Anymore", and his determination "To Make America Great Again" that rallied his supporters, and that affirms the national image that is part of their self-identity. The news media and Trump's opponents never understood why their mocking question, 'what does that mean', about Trumps slogan, 'Make America Great Again' never gained any traction—it was because Trump's supporters knew exactly what it meant.

Trump v. Status Quo

• • •

Institutional reform is extremely difficult thing to bring
about, and there is no guarantee that it will be accomplished
without a major disruption of the political order.

FRANCIS FUKUYAMA

THE TRUMP SAGA CONTINUES, BUT the result of the general election
cannot rewrite the story of Trump's nomination. It is a remarkable
story of an extraordinary individual with no political experience and
a bare-bones organization prevailing through the sheer force of his
personality and clarity of purpose over all the social forces society
could array against him. And Trump didn't just prevail: he won the
Republican nomination with more votes than any other candidate in
history and did it spending less in 2016 dollars than Romney spent
eight years earlier in 2008 dollars.

The reasons Trump won the Republican nomination define who
Trump's real opponents in the general election are. They are not
Hillary Clinton and the Democrats, but the entire political class
that includes the political news media—i.e. the status quo.

In his magisterial treatise on Political Order and Political Decay, Professor Francis Fukuyama wrote:

"Human beings make political choices at critical junctures in their history that force their societies onto very different trajectories for better or worse."[181]

America finds itself at such a juncture in its history, and the extraordinary story of Trump's nomination proves it. But what are these different trajectories, because they are most assuredly not determined by the policy differences between the two candidates.

Most of the public is aware of how daunting the collective problems facing the country are notwithstanding their jaunty mockery by a President determined to inflate his achievements in office when he is reminded of them. But there is something more fundamental confronting America than the economic, social and international problems besetting the country, and glib references to Washington's dysfunction by our media men does not inform the public of what that is: it merely reminds it that the political media, the Fourth Estate and a vital organ of government, is also dysfunctional.

The role of the political media is to provide citizens with the information they need to make decisions about their lives and their government. In this election cycle, that means informing the public of why Washington is so dysfunctional, and what it would take to correct the dysfunction, so that people can more rationally choose which candidate is more likely to implement the changes required. Far from fulfilling this role, the main stream media and cable news networks are actually putting their thumbs on the electoral scales far

---

181 Fukuyama, supra note 177 at 270 (page 201).

more than they have done in the past, and have gone all out to destroy Trump's candidacy and ensure that Hillary Clinton is elected.

Political ideas drive social change at opportune moments,[182] and the choice confronting voters in this election is who espouses ideas that can reform the institutional dysfunction tearing apart the fabric of American society: Trump or the political establishment represented by Hillary Clinton. And the reason the vitriol against Trump is so ferocious is that he is challenging political ideas that

"thrive on human emotions, generating rage, fear enthusiasm, love, sacrifice, altruism, mass murder, torture and rape, much in same way as religious doctrines have run the gamut of human virtues and vices".[183]

The problem confronting America is so serious because the political dysfunction is systemic, not contingent—that is, it does not dependent on who happens to be in the White House, but on special interests and their lobbyists, and politicians on both sides of the aisle. These political elites have captured the institutions of government and have no interest in reforming a system from which they benefit, indeed, many depend on entirely.

This simple fact explains the most extraordinary aspect of the Trump phenomenon—that he was opposed not just by the media and the Democrats, but by members of his own party. That prominent Republicans have publicly declared their intention to vote for Hillary

---

182 Manfred B. Steger, The Rise of the Global Imaginary, Oxford University Press, New York, 2008
183 Id. at 4.

Clinton is the surest manifestation that political elites would rather maintain the status quo, even if it meant them being out of power in the immediate future, than reform the system.

It also explains the ferocity of the opposition to Trump: he is not invested in the system or dependent on any lobby within that system, as his nomination proved. He is, therefore, uniquely placed to unite and lead a coalition of out-groups that it will take to reform the system—and this terrifies the political in-groups.

So the political choice facing the nation in this election is whether to continue on the present trajectory with Hillary Clinton or chose a completely new trajectory with Donald Trump. If the country chooses Hillary Clinton, it will commit itself to entrenching further the neo-patrimonial clientelism—otherwise referred to as a special-interest oligarchy— that has infected American politics, and make even decisions that everyone wants, like tax reform, impossible because they are so easy for a few to block.

So the threat of a Hillary Clinton presidency lies not in the unforeseeable consequences of the foreseeably corrupt administration she would lead, but the perpetuation of institutional dysfunction and further political decay at a time when political and social instability plagues many parts of the world, and the Sword of Damocles hangs over the international balance of power.

If, on the other hand, the country chooses Donald Trump, it will be banking that this extraordinary man can by the sheer force of his personality, drive and determination, using his experience of successfully managing diverse organizations and people can reform the Washington bureaucracy— by making meritocratic rather than

political appointments to government and the diplomatic service—
because he is beholden to no one.

It would be an experiment, to be sure, but as one of its greatest
justices reminded the nation, *'all of life is an experiment'*.[184]

The last gasp attempt of those who created the Washington dysfunction that Hillary Clinton represents—politicians on both sides of
the aisle as well as special interests and their lobbyists—is to convince
the public that this experiment is too dangerous to embark on because
Trump does not have the right temperament. But it is a very specious
argument, for the threat of a Trump presidency is entirely illusory.

For one thing, the power of an American president to take drastic,
undemocratic actions unilaterally is non-existent under our system of
checks and balances. Indeed, according to Professor Fukuyama and
others, these checks and balances has created the 'vetocracy' that is responsible for Washington's dysfunction. For another thing, bombastic
domestic political language has never had any geopolitical affect or
caused any international incident in history that I am aware of. And, in
any case, much of what Trump is supposed to have said is only in the
minds of media men and members of the political class opposing him.

However much the likes of General Hayden, former Director
of the National Security Agency and CIA, may want to impute responsibility to speakers for how others interpret what they say,[185] no
father who tells a reporter, *"my son has grown another foot"*, should be
held accountable for a news story about 'A Three-Legged Boy'.

---

184 Abrams v. United States, 250 U.S. 616 (1919).
185 http://www.wsj.com/articles/donald-trump-says-second-amendment-people-can-
stop-hillary-clinton-from-curbing-gun-rights-1470773378